Electoral Systems
and Conflict

in Divided Societies

Ben Reilly and Andrew Reynolds

Papers on International Conflict Resolution
No. 2

Committee on International Conflict Resolution

Commission on Behavioral and Social Sciences and Education

National Research Council

NATIONAL ACADEMY PRESS
Washington, D.C. 1999

NATIONAL ACADEMY PRESS • 2101 Constitution Ave., N.W. • Washington, DC 20418

NOTICE: The project that is the subject of this report was approved by the Governing Board of the National Research Council, whose members are drawn from the councils of the National Academy of Sciences, the National Academy of Engineering, and the Institute of Medicine. The members of the committee responsible for the report were chosen for their special competences and with regard for appropriate balance.

The National Academy of Sciences is a private, nonprofit, self-perpetuating society of distinguished scholars engaged in scientific and engineering research, dedicated to the furtherance of science and technology and to their use for the general welfare. Upon the authority of the charter granted to it by the Congress in 1863, the Academy has a mandate that requires it to advise the federal government on scientific and technical matters. Dr. Bruce M. Alberts is president of the National Academy of Sciences.

The National Academy of Engineering was established in 1964, under the charter of the National Academy of Sciences, as a parallel organization of outstanding engineers. It is autonomous in its administration and in the selection of its members, sharing with the National Academy of Sciences the responsibility for advising the federal government. The National Academy of Engineering also sponsors engineering programs aimed at meeting national needs, encourages education and research, and recognizes the superior achievements of engineers. Dr. William A. Wulf is president of the National Academy of Engineering.

The Institute of Medicine was established in 1970 by the National Academy of Sciences to secure the services of eminent members of appropriate professions in the examination of policy matters pertaining to the health of the public. The Institute acts under the responsibility given to the National Academy of Sciences by its congressional charter to be an adviser to the federal government and, upon its own initiative, to identify issues of medical care, research, and education. Dr. Kenneth I. Shine is president of the Institute of Medicine.

The National Research Council was organized by the National Academy of Sciences in 1916 to associate the broad community of science and technology with the Academy's purposes of furthering knowledge and advising the federal government. Functioning in accordance with general policies determined by the Academy, the Council has become the principal operating agency of both the National Academy of Sciences and the National Academy of Engineering in providing services to the government, the public, and the scientific and engineering communities. The Council is administered jointly by both Academies and the Institute of Medicine. Dr. Bruce M. Alberts and Dr. William A. Wulf are chairman and vice chairman, respectively, of the National Research Council.

The project that is the subject of this paper was funded by the Carnegie Corporation of New York through Grant Number B 6083. Additional support for this publication was provided by the International Institute for Democracy and Electoral Assistance. Any opinions, findings, conclusions, or recommendations expressed in this publication are those of the authors and do not necessarily reflect the view of the organizations or agencies that provided support for this project.

International Standard Book Number 0-309-06446-5

Additional copies of this report are available from National Academy Press, 2101 Constitution Avenue N.W., Lockbox 285, Washington, D.C. 20055; (800) 624-6242 or (202) 334-3313 (in the Washington metropolitan area); this report is also available online at http://www.nap.edu

Printed in the United States of America

COMMITTEE ON INTERNATIONAL CONFLICT RESOLUTION

Alexander L. George *(Chair)*, Department of Political Science, Stanford University
Juergen Dedring, Graduate Center, City University of New York
Francis M. Deng, Brookings Institution, Washington, DC
Ronald J. Fisher, Department of Psychology, University of Saskatchewan
James E. Goodby, U.S. Department of State, Washington, DC
Robert H. Mnookin, School of Law, Harvard University
Raymond Shonholtz, Partners for Democratic Change, San Francisco
Janice G. Stein, Department of Political Science, University of Toronto
Stanley J. Tambiah, Department of Anthropology, Harvard University
M. Crawford Young, Department of Political Science, University of Wisconsin, Madison
I. William Zartman, School of Advanced International Studies, Johns Hopkins University

Paul C. Stern, *Study Director*, National Research Council
Daniel Druckman, *Consultant*, George Mason University
Heather Schofield, *Senior Project Assistant*, National Research Council

Preface

This paper is one of a series being prepared for the National Research Council's Committee on International Conflict Resolution. The committee was organized in late 1995 to respond to a growing need for prevention, management, and resolution of violent conflict in the international arena, a concern about the changing nature and context of such conflict in the post-Cold War era, and a recent expansion of knowledge in the field.

The committee's main goal is to advance the practice of conflict resolution by using the methods and critical attitude of science to examine the effectiveness of various techniques and concepts that have been advanced for preventing, managing, and resolving international conflicts. The committee's research agenda has been designed to supplement the work of other groups, particularly the Carnegie Corporation of New York's Commission on Preventing Deadly Conflict, which issued its final report in December 1997. The committee has identified a number of specific techniques and concepts of current interest to policy practitioners and has asked leading specialists on each one to carefully review and analyze available knowledge and to summarize what is known about the conditions under which each is or is not effective. These papers present the results of their work.

Each paper in the series attempts to address important practical questions by testing conventional wisdom against experience, identifying critical issues, making concepts clearer, and summarizing the lessons of experience. In the committee's judgment, such analysis will help conflict resolution practitioners in governments, international organizations, nongovernmental organizations, and academic centers to diagnose conflict situations and make better informed choices about whether, when, and how to intervene.

The committee recognizes the great difficulties inherent in any effort to draw conclusions about the effects of interventions in historical processes. We nevertheless believe that these papers, by virtue of their thorough and critical examination of the relevant evidence, will add appreciably to practitioners' understanding. They will also advance a second goal of the committee, which is to improve the quality of future analytical efforts to understand international conflict and conflict resolution.

We express our appreciation to the Carnegie Corporation of New York for its generous support of the committee's activities and to the International Institute for Democracy and Electoral Assistance for support for the separate publication of this work. We thank Ben Reilly and Andrew Reynolds for their work on this paper. We also express our appreciation to the many practitioners and scholars who contributed to this effort by granting interviews, participating in a seminar to discuss an early version of the paper, or formally reviewing drafts. We also thank Heather Schofield, who has managed the logistics of this project from its inception, and James Ryan, who did the copy editing.

> Alexander L. George, *Chair*
> Paul C. Stern, *Study Director*
> Committee on International Conflict Resolution

Papers on
International Conflict Resolution

This paper is one of a series being prepared for the National Research Council's Committee on International Conflict Resolution. When the series is completed, the papers will be published in a volume, tentatively entitled *International Conflict Resolution: Techniques And Evaluation*. The expected contents are listed below.

NONTRADITIONAL FORMS IN
CONFLICT RESOLUTION

STRUCTURAL APPROACHES TO CONFLICT IN
DIVIDED STATES

CONCLUSIONS

Electoral Systems
and Conflict
in Divided Societies

Electoral Systems and Conflict in Divided Societies

Ben Reilly and Andrew Reynolds[1]

INTRODUCTION

This work examines whether the choice of an electoral system in a culturally plural society can affect the potential for future violent conflict. We find that it can, but that there is no single electoral system that is likely to be best for all divided societies. We distinguish four basic strategies of electoral system design. The optimal choice for peacefully managing conflict depends on several identifiable factors specific to the country, including the way and degree to which ethnicity is politicized, the intensity of conflict, and the demographic and geographic distribution of ethnic groups. In addition, the electoral system that is most appropriate for initially ending internal conflict may not be the best one for longer-term conflict management. In short, while electoral systems can be powerful levers for shaping the content and practice of politics in divided societies, their design is highly sensitive to context. Consideration of the relationship between these variables and the operation of different electoral systems enables the development of contingent generalizations that can assist policymakers in the field of electoral system design.

Several fundamental assumptions that underlie the thinking of many Western policy specialists are called into question by the evidence assembled here concerning the relationship between conflict and elections. The first assumption, derived from Western experience, is that "free and fair elections" are the most appropriate way both to avoid and to manage acute internal conflict in other countries. The second assumption, which goes hand in hand with the first, is the implicit approval of "winner take all" models of both government and election and disapproval of arrangements that emphasize power-sharing and cooperation. The third, again derived from Western experience, is that the types of electoral systems used in the West can be successfully transplanted to the developing world. A final assumption is that stable democracies need to be based on a system of individual rights rather than group rights. This work, to varying degrees, calls all of these assumptions into question.

The multi-country evidence cited here offers some insights about how to diagnose a country's situation for the purpose of selecting an electoral system that can help that country address its communal conflicts peacefully. Realistic diagnosis of key social-structural issues is a necessary precondition to designing a successful system. In practice, there is little evidence of such diagnosis at work in the historical record. Moreover, the choice of an electoral system involves tradeoffs among a number of desirable attributes. Thus, the role of local actors, who can draw both on international experience and on their knowledge of domestic conditions and priorities, is key.

Institutions, Conflict Management, and Democracy

The study of political institutions is integral to the study of democratization because institutions constitute and sustain democracies:[2] as Scarritt and Mozaffar succinctly summarize, "to craft democracies is to craft institutions" (1996:3). Perhaps most important for newly democratizing countries is the way that institutions shape the choices available to political actors. Koelble notes that this emphasis on "rules, structures, codes, and organizational norms" is based upon Weber's view of organizations as constructs designed to distribute rewards and sanctions and to establish guidelines for acceptable types of behavior (1995:233). March and Olsen argue that "constitutions, laws, contracts, and customary rules of politics make many potential actions or considerations illegitimate or unnoticed; some alternatives are excluded from the agenda before politics begins, but these constraints are not imposed full-blown by an external social system; they develop within the context of political institutions" (1984:740). In his important 1991 book *Democracy and the Market*, Adam Przeworski develops a concept of democracy as "rule open-endedness or organized uncertainty . . . and the less the uncertainty over potential outcomes the lower the incentive for groups to organize institutionally" (1991:13). Thus his influential conclusion, central to the spirit of this paper, that was a recognition that democratic government, rather than oligarchy or authoritarianism, presented by far the best prospects for managing deep societal divisions, and that democracy itself operates as a system for *managing* and *processing* rather than resolving conflict.[3]

In their preface to *Politics in Developing Countries*, Larry Diamond, Juan Linz, and Seymour Martin Lipset argue that institutions influence political stability in four important respects:

(i) Because they structure behavior into stable, predictable, and recurrent patterns, institutionalized systems are less volatile and more enduring, and so are institutionalized democracies.

(ii) Regardless of how they perform economically, democracies that have more coherent and effective political institutions will be more likely to perform well politically in maintaining not only political order but also a rule of law, thus ensuring civil liberties, checking the abuse of power, and providing meaningful representation, competition, choice, and accountability.

(iii) Over the long run well-institutionalized democracies are also more likely to produce workable, sustainable, and effective economic and social policies because they have more effective and stable structures for representing interests and they are more likely to produce working congressional majorities or coalitions that can adopt and sustain policies.

Lastly, (iv) democracies that have capable, coherent democratic institutions are better able to limit military involvement in politics and assert civilian control over the military (1995:33).

Institutions and Democratization in the Developing World

While accepting that throughout the developing world the societal constraints on democracy are considerable, such constraints still leave room for conscious political strategies which may further or hamper successful democratization. As a result, institutions work not just at the margins, but are central to the structuring of stability, particularly in ethnically heterogeneous societies. Scarritt and Mozaffar push the critical role of institutions even further by arguing that distinct institutional arrangements not only distinguish democracies, but invest governments with different abilities to manage conflicts, and thus that the survival of third-wave democracies under extremely adverse conditions often hinges on these institutional differences (1996:3).

Institutional design takes on an enhanced role in newly democratizing and divided societies because, in the absence of other structures, politics becomes the primary mode of communication between divergent social forces. In any society, groups (collections of individuals who identify some sort of mutual bond) talk to each other—sometimes about resolving distributive conflicts, sometimes about planning for the national future, and often about more mundane issues of everyday concern. In the pluralist democracies of the West, there are a variety of channels of communication open through which to carry on these conversations. Individuals from different cultures and perspectives can communicate with each other through the institutions of civil society via the press, social and sporting clubs, residence associations, church groups, labor unions, and so on.[4]

In fledgling democracies, however, where society is more deeply divided along ethnic, regional, or religious lines, political institutions take on even greater importance. They become the most prominent, and often the only, channel of communication between disparate groups. Such societies do not yet have the mixed institutions which characterize a broad civil society. Sporting, social, and religious groups are rigidly segregated, and various peoples do not live together, play together, or really talk to each other. Similarly, many new democracies do not yet have a vigorous free press where groups can talk. This holds true in the West as well, where different media outlets speak to different social groups or classes, and where cities are often segregated along racial, ethnic, and economic lines; but divided societies in the developing world often represent the extreme of the continuum, and that is why political institutions exist as the primary channel of communication.

Because political institutions fulfill this role as the preeminent method of communication, they must facilitate communication channels between groups who need to talk. If they exclude people from coming to the table, then their conflicts can only be solved through force, not through negotiation and mutual accommodation. Further, those doing the talking, the representatives, must be just that—representative. To be able to make promises and then deliver on them, each political representative needs to be accountable to his or her constituency to the highest degree possible through institutional rules. The extent to which institutional rules place a premium on the representational roles of such figures, or rather seek to break down the overall salience of ethnicity by forcing them to transcend their status as representatives of only one group or another, is central to the scholarly debate about political institutions in deeply divided societies.

The Validity of Constitutional Engineering

There is little dispute that institutions *matter*, but there is much greater dispute regarding how much one can (or would wish to) engineer political outcomes through the choice of institutional structures. In this regard there exists an important distinction between an *institutional choice* approach and those who seek institutional innovation through *constitutional engineering* to mitigate conflict within divided societies. Sisk notes that "there has been an implicit assumption by scholars of comparative politics who specialize in divided societies that such political conflict can be potentially ameliorated if only such societies would adopt certain types of democratic institutions, that is, through 'political engineering'" (1995:5). Indeed, Horowitz proposes that "whatever their preferences, it remains true that a severely divided society needs a heavy dose—on the engineering analogy, even a redundant dose—of institutions laden with incentives to accommodation" (1991:280-281). Similarly, Sartori argues that "the organization of the state requires more than any other organization to be kept on course by a structure of rewards and punishments, of 'good' inducements and scary deterrents" (1994:203).

However, Sisk runs counter to Horowitz, Lijphart, Sartori, and others in arguing that constitutional engineering should not be the primary focus of research: "most scholarship about democracy in divided societies centers too much on examining the best outcomes, as opposed to looking at the ways these outcomes evolve through bargaining processes" (1995:18). Indeed, Elster supports Sisk with the view that "it is impossible to predict with certainty or even qualified probability the consequences of a major constitutional change" (1988:304). Elster and Sisk remain in the minority on this question, given that most comparative political scientists would be happy to predict with 'qualified probability' the results of a shift in electoral law or democratic system. As Sartori correctly notes, if we follow Elster's somewhat defeatist logic, then "the practical implication of the inability of predicting is the inability of reforming" (1994:200). There seems little reason to give up the potential power of institutions for conflict resolution if we are confident of some degree of predictive ability when it comes to institutional consequences.

Ultimately, there is a temporal dimension to both constitutional design and the politics of institutional choice. Political actors in a fledgling democracy may choose certain structures (rationally) because they maximize their gain in the short term. Thus, negotiators may not alight upon more inclusive structures recommended by political scientists posing as constitutional engineers. However, the promise of constitutional engineering rests on the assumption that long-term sociopolitical stability is the nation's overarching goal; and the institutions needed to facilitate that goal may not be the same as those which provide maximum short-term gain to the negotiating actors in the transitional period. Thus, *institutional choice* and *constitutional engineering* are, in practice, compatible approaches. One seeks to understand what drives short-term bargains, while the other seeks to offer more long-term solutions with the benefit of comparative cross-national evidence. The task of the constitutional engineer is not only to find which institutional package will most likely ensure democratic consolidation, but to persuade those domestic politicians making the decisions that they should choose long-term stability over short-term gain.

Electoral Engineering and Conflict Management

The set of democratic institutions a nation adopts is thus integral to the long-term prospects of any new regime as they structure the rules of the game of political competition. Within the range of democratic institutions, many scholars have argued that there is no more important choice than which electoral system is to be used. Electoral systems have long been recognized as one of the most important institutional mechanisms for shaping the nature of political competition, first, because they are, to quote one electoral authority, "the most specific manipulable instrument of politics"[5]—that is, they can be purposively designed to achieve particular outcomes—and second, because they structure the arena of political competition, including the party system; offer incentives to behave in certain ways; and reward those who respond to these incentives with electoral success. The great potential of electoral system design for influencing political behavior is thus that it can reward particular types of behavior and place constraints on others. This is why electoral system design has been seized upon by many scholars (Lijphart, 1977, 1994; Sartori, 1968; Taagepera and Shugart, 1989; Horowitz, 1985, 1991) as one of the chief levers of constitutional engineering to be used in mitigating conflict within divided societies. As Lijphart notes, "If one wants to change the nature of a particular democracy, the electoral system is likely to be the most suitable and effective instrument for doing so" (1995a:412). Nevertheless, the fact that electoral system design has not proved to be a panacea for the vagaries of communal conflict in many places has shed some doubt upon the primacy that electoral systems are given as "tools of conflict management." What we attempt to do in this paper is assess the cumulative evidence of the relationship between electoral systems and intrasocietal conflict, and determine under what conditions electoral systems have the most influence on outcomes.

An electoral system is designed to do three main jobs. First, it translates the votes cast into seats won in a legislative chamber. The system may give more weight to proportionality between votes cast and seats won, or it may funnel the votes (however fragmented among parties) into a parliament which contains two large parties representing polarized views. Second, electoral systems act as the conduit through which the people can hold their elected representatives accountable. Third, different electoral systems serve to structure the boundaries of "acceptable" political discourse in different ways, and give incentives for those competing for power to couch their appeals to the electorate in distinct ways. In terms of deeply ethnically divided societies, for example, where ethnicity represents a fundamental political cleavage, particular electoral systems can reward candidates and parties who act in a cooperative, accommodatory manner to rival groups; or they can punish these candidates and instead reward those who appeal only to their own ethnic group. However, the "spin" which an electoral system gives to the system is ultimately contextual and will depend on the specific cleavages and divisions within any given society.

That said, it is important not to overestimate the power of elections and electoral systems to resolve deep-rooted enmities and bring conflictual groups into a stable and institutionalized political system which processes conflict through democratic rather than violent means. Some analysts have argued that while established democracies have evolved structures which process disputes in ways that successfully avoid "conflict," newly democratizing states are considerably more likely to experience civil or national violence (see Mansfield and Snyder, 1995). The argument that competitive multiparty elections actually exacerbate ethnic polarism has been marshaled by a number of African leaders (for example, Yoweri Museveni in Uganda and Daniel arap Moi in Kenya) in defense of their hostility to multiparty democracy. And it is true to say that "elections, as competitions among individuals, parties, and their ideas are inherently just that: competitive. Elections are, and are meant to be polarizing; they seek to highlight social choices" (Reynolds and Sisk, 1998:18). Elections may be "the defining moment", but while some founding elections have forwarded the twin causes of democratization and conflict resolution, such as South Africa and Mozambique, others have gone seriously awry, such as Angola and Burundi.

While it is important not to overemphasize the importance or influence of political institutions (and particularly of electoral systems) as factors influencing democratic transitions, it is more common when dealing with developing countries that the reverse is true: scholars and policy makers alike have typically given too much attention to social forces and not enough to the careful crafting of appropriate democratic institutions by which those forces can be expressed. As Larry Diamond has argued, "the single most important and urgent factor in the consolidation of democracy is not civil society but political institutionalization."[6] To survive, democracies in developing countries need above all "robust political institutions" such as secure executives and effective legislatures composed of coherent, broadly based parties encouraged by aggregative electoral institutions.[7] We thus return to the underlying premise of constitutional engineering as it relates to electoral system design: while it is true that elections are merely one cog in the wheel of a much broader framework of institutional arrangements, sociohistorical pressures, and strategic actor behaviors, at the same time electoral systems are an indispensable and integral part of this broader framework. One electoral system might nurture accommodatory tendencies which already exist, while another may make it far more rational for ethnic entrepreneurs to base their appeals on exclusionary notions of ethnochauvinism.

What the collective evidence from elections held in divided societies does seem to suggest is that an appropriately crafted electoral system can do some good in nurturing accommodative tendencies, but the implementation of an inappropriate system can do severe harm to the trajectory of conflict resolution and democratization in a plural state (see Reilly, 1997a; Reynolds and Sisk, 1998). Given this, is it possible to outline criteria that one might use to judge the success or failure of any given electoral system design? In light of the multicausal nature of institutions, democracy, and political behavior, it would be foolhardy to say with absolute certainty that a particular electoral system was solely, or even primarily, responsible for a change—for better or worse—in ethnic relations in a divided society. Nevertheless, with the benefit of a holistic view of a nation's democratization process, it is possible to highlight instances where the electoral system itself appears to have encouraged accommodation, and those where it played a part in exaggerating the incentives for ethnic polarization. We hope that the typologies and analytical tools introduced in this paper as part of a contingent theory of electoral system design may help future research elucidate such electoral system effects.

Our Knowledge to Date

To date, our academic knowledge of electoral systems and their consequences has been predominantly based upon the more generic and abstract study of electoral systems as decision-making rules, structuring games played by faceless "rational actors" in environments which are often devoid of historical, socioeconomic, and cultural context. A comprehensive body of work exists which points to the mathematical effects of various systems on party systems, proportionality, and government formation (see, for example, Farrell, 1997; Grofman and Lijphart, 1986; Lijphart and Grofman, 1984; Lijphart, 1994; Rae, 1967; and Taagepera and Shugart, 1989). This is not to deride those very important works—and the discipline as a whole—rather it reflects the fact that much less work has been carried out on the subject of electoral systems, democratization, and conflict resolution. In addition, the majority of work on electoral systems to date has exhibited both a strong bias toward the study of established democracies in the West, and has been mostly country specific. This paper seeks to give a fillip to the increasingly important and more truly comparative study of how electoral systems can be crafted to improve the lot of divided societies.

Historically, Huntington has identified three periods in which each contained a "wave" of transitions of states from nondemocracy to multiparty competition (Huntington, 1991). Each wave saw the crafting of new constitutions for a new order, and electoral systems were regularly the most controversial and debated aspect of the new institutions. Huntington's "first wave" takes in the period from 1828 to 1926 when the United States, Great Britain, Australia, Canada, New Zealand, and a number of smaller European states began to evolve degrees of multiparty competition and "democratic" institutional structures. The debates over electoral systems (especially in Scandinavia and continental Europe) during this first wave of democratization mirrored many of the debates that new democracies are experiencing in the 1990s—the perceived trade-offs between "accountability" and "representativeness," between a close geographical link between elector and representative and proportionality for parties in parliament (see Carstairs, 1980). Huntington's second wave encompasses the post-second world war period through the decolonization decades of the 1950s and early 1960s. This wave saw many states either inherit or receive electoral systems designed and promoted by outside powers. West Germany, Austria, Japan, and Korea are examples of such "external imposition" by Allied powers in the postwar period, while virtually all the fleetingly democratic postcolonial nation states of Africa and Asia inherited direct transplants of the electoral and constitutional systems of their colonial masters.

Finally, the "third wave" of democratization, which began with the overthrow of the Salazar dictatorship in Portugal in 1974 and continues on to this day, gives us a wealth of case study material when it comes to assessing electoral system design in new democracies and those societies divided by cultural or social hostilities. In 1997, Reynolds and Reilly found only seven countries (out of 212 independent states and related territories) which did not hold direct elections for their legislatures, and of those 98 were classified as "free" on the basis of political rights and civil liberties in the 1995-1996 Freedom House *Freedom in the World* (Reynolds and Reilly, 1997). Therefore, we can be confident that a considerable range of comparative material is available for a study of how electoral systems influence democratization and stability in divided societies. This is even more so if we are mindful not to ignore the important lessons of nineteenth-century emerging democracies such as the British dominions (Canada, Australia, South Africa, New Zealand), with their divisions between and within "settler" and "indigenous" groups, or the multiethnic societies of continental Europe (Belgium, Austria-Hungary, Switzerland, the Netherlands, and Luxembourg), which fulfilled many of the classic elements of "plural" or "divided" societies at the turn of the century. In both groups, electoral system design was seen as a means of dealing with divisions and, particularly in the European examples, as a tool of accommodation-building between potentially hostile religious or linguistic groups.

DEVELOPING AN ANALYTICAL FRAMEWORK FOR A CONTINGENT THEORY OF ELECTORAL SYSTEM DESIGN

Consultants on electoral system design rightly shy away from the "one-size-fits-all" approach of recommending one system for all contexts. Indeed, when asked to identify their "favorite" or "best" system, constitutional experts will say "it depends" and the dependents are more often than not variables such as: What does the society look like? How is it divided? Do ethnic or communal divides dovetail with voting behavior? Do different groups live geographically intermixed or segregated? What is the country's political history? Is it an established democracy, a transitional democracy, or a redemocratizing state? What are the broader constitutional arrangements that the legislature is working within?

Historically, the process of electoral system design has tended to occur on a fragmented case-by-case basis, which has led to the inevitable and continual reinvention of the wheel because of limited comparative information. In this paper, we seek to develop an analytical framework upon which a contingent theory of electoral system design may be built. When assessing the appropriateness of any given electoral system for a divided society, three variables become particularly salient:

(1) knowledge of *the nature of societal division* is paramount (i.e., the nature of group identity, the intensity of conflict, the nature of the dispute, and the spatial distribution of conflictual groups);

(2) the nature of the *political system* (i.e., the nature of the state, the party system, and the overall constitutional framework); and

(3) the *process* which led to the adoption of the electoral system (i.e., was the system inherited from a colonial power, was it consciously designed, was it externally imposed, or did it emerge through a process of evolution and unintended consequences).

In the following section we describe these three key variables and then operationalize them in the conclusion.

Nature of Societal Division

The Nature of Group Identity

As noted earlier, appropriate constitutional design is ultimately contextual and rests on the nuances of a nation's unique social cleavages. The nature of division within a society is revealed in part by the extent to which ethnicity correlates with party support and voting behavior. And that factor will often determine whether institutional engineering is able to dissipate ethnic conflicts or merely contain them. There are two dimensions to *the nature of group identity*: one deals with foundations (i.e., whether the society divided along racial, ethnic, ethnonationalistic, religious, regional, linguistic, etc. lines), while the second deals with how rigid and entrenched such divisions are. Scholarship on the latter subject has developed a continuum with the rigidity of received identity (i.e., primordialism) on one side and the malleability of constructed social identities (i.e., constructivist or instrumentalist) on the other (see Shils, 1957; Geertz, 1973; Young, 1976; Anderson, 1991; Newman, 1991; Esman, 1994).

Clearly, if ethnic allegiances are indeed primordial, and therefore rigid, then a specific type of power sharing, based on an electoral system which primarily recognizes and accommodates interests based on ascriptive communal traits rather than individual ideological ones, is needed to manage competing claims for scarce resources. If ethnic identities and voting behaviors are fixed, then there is no space for institutional incentives aimed at promoting accommodatory strategies to work. Nevertheless, while it is true that in almost all multiethnic societies there are indeed correlations between voting behavior and ethnicity, the causation is far more complex. It is far from clear that primordial ethnicity, the knee-jerk reaction to vote for "your group's party" regardless of other factors, is the chief explanation of these correlations. More often than not ethnicity has become a proxy for other things, a semiartificial construct which has its roots in community but has been twisted out of all recognition. This is what Robert Price calls the antagonistic "politics of communalism"—ethnicity which has been politicized and exploited to serve entrepreneurial ends (1995).

In practice, virtually every example of politicized ethnic conflict exhibits claims based on a combination of both "primordial" historical associations and "instrumentalized" opportunistic adaptations.[8] In the case of Sierra Leone, for example, Kandeh (1992) has shown that dominant local elites, masquerading as "cultural politicians," shaped and mobilized ethnicity to serve their interests. In Uganda, President Museveni has used the "fear of tribalism" as an excuse to avoid multipartism. Nevertheless, in both the colonial and postcolonial "one-party state" eras, strategies to control and carve up the Ugandan state were based upon the hostile mobilization of ethnic and religious identities. Malawi acts as a counterfactual to the primordial ethnicity thesis and offers an example of how political affiliations play out differently when incentive structures are altered. In the multiparty elections of 1994, a history of colonial rule, missionary activity, and Hastings Banda's "Chewa-ization" of national culture combined together to plant the seeds of conflictual regionalism which both dovetailed with, and cut across, preconceived ethnic boundaries. The south voted for the United Democratic Front of Bakili Muluzi, the Center for the Malawi Congress Party of Banda, and the north for the Alliance for Democracy led by Chakufwa Chihana. But voting patterns depended more upon region than ethnicity. Kaspin notes that "not only did non-Tumbuka in the north vote for AFORD, and non-Yao in the south vote for the UDF, but non-Tumbuka and non-Yao groups divided by regional borders tended to support the opposition candidates of their own region" (1995:614).[9]

If ethnic conflict is not predetermined, or is more often a proxy for other interests, then incentives can be laid for other cleavages to emerge as ethnic divides becomes less salient. In South Africa, for example, the rules of the game encouraged parties to appeal across ethnic boundaries. As Price (1995) notes, South Africa has been remarkably free of ethnic conflict in the postapartheid period, bearing in mind its history of repressive racial laws. Challenging conventional wisdom, he argues that, "the South African case is important for the contemporary study of ethnicity in politics precisely because it is an ethnically heterogeneous society *without* significant ethnic conflict." The election of April 1994 also lent credence to the claim that the inclusive institutional incentives of the interim constitution helped make politicized ethnicity far less salient. All parties (bar the Afrikaner Freedom Front and the National Party in the Western Cape) strived to appeal across ethnic divides, and the African National Congress (ANC), National Party (NP), Inkatha Freedom Party (IFP), DP, and PAC presented multiethnic and multiracial lists of parliamentary candidates. In a 1994 postelection survey, Robert Mattes (1995) of the Institute for Democracy in South Africa found only 3 percent of voters claimed to have based their political affiliations on ethnic identity.[10]

Intensity of Conflict

A second variable in terms of the nature of any given conflict and its susceptibility to electoral engineering is simply the intensity and depth of hostility between the competing groups. It is worth remembering that, although academic and international attention is naturally drawn to extreme cases, most ethnic conflicts do *not* degenerate into all-out civil war (Fearon and Laitin, 1996). While few societies are entirely free from multiethnic antagonism, most are able to manage to maintain a degree of mutual accommodation sufficient to avoid state collapse. There are numerous examples of quite deeply divided states in which the various groups maintain frosty but essentially civil relations between one another despite a considerable degree of mutual antipathy—such as the relations between Malays, Chinese, and Indians in Malaysia, for example. There are other cases (e.g., Sri Lanka) where what appeared to be a relatively benign interethnic environment and less pronounced racial cleavages nonetheless broke down into violent armed conflict, but where democratic government has nonetheless been the rule more than the exception. And then, of course, there are the cases of utter breakdown in relations and the "ethnic cleansing" of one group by another, typified most recently and horribly by Bosnia.

The significance of these examples is that each of these states are deeply divided, but the different intensity of the conflict means that different electoral "levers" would need to be considered in each case. Malaysia has been able to use a majoritarian electoral system which utilizes a degree of "vote pooling" and power-sharing to manage relations between the major ethnic groups—a successful strategy in terms of managing ethnic relations there, but possible only because Chinese voters are prepared, under the right circumstances, to vote for Malay candidates and vice versa. By contrast, under the "open list" proportional representation (PR) system used for parliamentary elections in Sri Lanka, research has found that Sinhalese voters will, if given the chance, deliberately move Tamil candidates placed in a winnable position on a party list to a lower position—a factor which may well have occurred in South Africa as well, had not the electoral system used been a "closed" list, which allowed major parties such as the ANC and the NP to place ethnic minorities and women high on their party list. But even in Sri Lanka, the electoral system for Presidential elections allows Tamils and other minorities to indicate who their least-disliked Sinhalese candidate is—a system which has seen the election of ethnic moderates to the position of President at every election to date (Reilly, 1997b).

Contrast this with a case like Bosnia, where relations between ethnic groups are so deeply hostile that it is almost inconceivable that electors of one group would be prepared to vote for others under any circumstances. There, the 1996 transitional elections were contested overwhelmingly by ethnically based parties, with minimal contact between competing parties, and with any accommodation between groups having to take place *after* the election—in negotiations between ethnic elites representing the various groups—rather than before. The problem with such an approach is that it assumes that elites themselves are willing to behave moderately to their opponents, when much of the evidence from places like Bosnia tends directly to contradict such an assumption. We will return to this problem, which bedevils elite-centered strategies for conflict management, later in this paper.

The Nature of the Dispute

Electoral system design is not merely contingent upon the basis and intensity of social cleavages but also, to some extent, upon the nature of the dispute which is manifested from cultural differences. The classic issue of dispute is the issue of group rights and status in a "multiethnic democracy," i.e., a system characterized both by democratic decision-making institutions and by the presence of two or more ethnic groups, defined as a group of people who see themselves as a distinct cultural community; who often share a common language, religion, kinship, and/ or physical characteristics (such as skin color); and who tend to harbor negative and hostile feelings toward members of other groups.[11] The majority of this paper deals with this fundamental cleavage of ethnicity.

Other types of disputes often dovetail with ethnic ones, however. If the issue that divides groups is resource-based, for example, then the way in which the national parliament is elected has particular importance as disputes are managed through the central government allocation of resources to various regions and peoples. In this case, an electoral system which facilitated a broadly inclusive parliament might be more successful than one which exaggerated majoritarian tendencies or ethnic, regional, or other cleavages. This requirement would still hold true if the dispute was primarily cultural (i.e., revolved around the protection of minority languages and culturally specific schooling), but other institutional mechanisms, such as cultural autonomy and minority vetoes, would be at least as influential in alleviating conflict. The range of mechanisms available to conflicting parties is thus likely to include questions of parliamentary rules, power-sharing arrangements, language policies, and various forms of devolution and autonomy (see Harris and Reilly, 1998).

Lastly, disputes over territory often require innovative institutional arrangements which go well beyond the positive spins that electoral systems can create. In Spain and Canada, asymmetrical arrangements for, respectively, the Basque and Quebec regions, have been used to try and dampen calls for secession, while federalism has been promoted as an institution of conflict management in countries as diverse as Germany, Nigeria, South Africa, and Switzerland. All of these arrangements have a direct impact upon the choice of an appropriate electoral system. An example is the distinction in federal systems between lower "representative" chambers of parliament and upper "deliberative" ones, which create very different types of demands on politicians and thus require different electoral system choices to work effectively.

Spatial Distribution of Conflictual Groups

A final consideration when looking at different electoral options concerns the spatial distribution of ethnic groups, and particularly their relative size, number, and degree of geographic concentration or dispersion. For one thing, it is often the case that the geographic distribution of conflicting groups is also related to the intensity of conflict between them. The frequent intergroup contact facilitated by geographical intermixture may increase the levels of mutual hostility, but it is also likely to act as a moderating force against the most extreme manifestations of ethnic conflict.[12] Familiarity may breed contempt, but it also usually breeds a certain degree of acceptance as well. Intermixed groups are thus less likely to be in a state of all-out civil war than those that are territorially separated from one another.

Furthermore, intermixing gives rise to different ethnic agendas and desires. Territorial claims and self-determination rallying cries are more difficult to invoke when groups are widely dispersed and intermixed with each other. In such situations, group mobilization around issues such as civil or group rights and economic access is likely to be more prevalent.[13] Conversely, however, territorial separation is sometimes the only way to manage the most extreme types of ethnic conflict, which usually involves consideration of some type of formal territorial devolution of power or autonomy. In the extreme case of "ethnic cleansing" in Bosnia, areas which previously featured highly intermixed populations of Serbs, Croats, and Muslims are now predominantly mono-ethnic.

Another scenario is where the distribution of ethnic groups is such that some types of electoral system are naturally precluded. This is a function not of group size so much as the geographic concentration or dispersion of different communities. Any electoral strategy for conflict management needs to be tailored to the realities of political geography. Territorial prescriptions for federalism or other types of devolution of power will usually be a prominent concern, as will issues of group autonomy. Indigenous and/or tribal groups tend to display a particularly strong tendency toward geographical concentration. African minorities, for example, have been found to be more highly concentrated in single contiguous geographical areas than minorities in other regions, which means that many electoral constituencies and informal local power bases will be controlled by a single ethnopolitical group (Scarritt, 1993). This has considerable implications for electoral engineers: it means that any system of election that relies on single-member electoral will likely produce "ethnic fiefdoms" at the local level. Minority representation and/or power-sharing under these conditions would probably require some form of multimember district system and proportional representation.

Contrast this with the highly intermixed patterns of ethnic settlement found as a result of colonial settlement or labor importation and the vast Chinese and Indian diasporas found in some Asia-Pacific (e.g., Singapore, Fiji, Malaysia) and Caribbean (Guyana, Trinidad and Tobago) countries, in which members of various ethnic groups tend to be much more widely intermixed and, consequently, have more day-to-day contact. Here, ethnic identities are often mitigated by other cross-cutting cleavages, and even small single-member districts are likely to be ethnically heterogeneous, so that electoral systems which encourage parties to seek the support of different ethnic groups may well work to break down interethnic antagonisms and promote the development of broad, multiethnic parties. This situation requires a very different set of electoral procedures.

A final type of social structure involves extreme ethnic *multiplicity*, typically based upon the presence of many small, competing tribal groups—an unusual composition in Western states, but common in some areas of central Africa and the South Pacific—which typically requires strong local representation to function effectively. In the extreme case of Papua New Guinea, for example, there are several thousand competing clan groups speaking over 800 distinct languages (see Reilly, 1998a). Any attempt at proportional representation in such a case would be almost impossible, as it would require a parliament of several thousand members (and, because parties are either weak or nonexistent in almost all such cases, the usual party-based systems of proportional representation would be particularly inappropriate). This dramatically curtails the range of options available to electoral engineers.

Nature of Political System

Institutional prescriptions for electoral engineering also need to be mindful of the different political dynamics that distinguish transitional democracies from established ones. Transitional democracies, particularly those moving from a deep-rooted conflict situation, typically have a greater need for inclusiveness and a lower threshold for the robust rhetoric of adversarial politics than their established counterparts. Similarly, the stable political environments of most Western countries, where two or three main parties can often reasonably expect regular periods in office via alternation of power or shifting governing coalitions, are very different from the type of zero-sum politics which so often characterize divided societies. This is one of the reasons that "winner-take-all" electoral systems have so often been identified as a contributor to the breakdown of democracy in the developing world: such systems tend to lock out minorities from parliamentary representation and, in situations of ethnically based parties, can easily lead to the total dominance of one ethnic group over all others. Democracy, under these circumstances, can quickly become a situation of permanent inclusion and exclusion, a zero-sum game, with frightening results.

Electoral laws also affect the size and development of political parties. At least since Duverger, the conventional wisdom among electoral scholars has been that majoritarian electoral rules encourage the formation of a two-party system (and, by extension, one-party government), while proportional representation leads to a multiparty system (and coalition government). While there remains general agreement that majority systems tend to restrict the range of legislative representation and PR systems encourage it, the conventional wisdom of a causal relationship between an electoral system and a party system is increasingly looking out of date. In recent years, first-past-the-post (FPTP) has facilitated the fragmentation of the party system in established democracies such as Canada and India, while PR has seen the election of what look likely to be dominant single-party regimes in Namibia, South Africa, and elsewhere.

Just as electoral systems affect the formation of party systems, so party systems themselves have a major impact upon the shape of electoral laws. It is one of the basic precepts of political science that politicians and parties will make choices about institutions such as electoral systems that they think will benefit themselves. Different types of party system will thus tend to produce different electoral system choices. The best-known example of this is the adoption of PR in continental Europe in the early years of this century. The expansion of the franchise and the rise of powerful new social forces, such as the labor movement, prompted the adoption of systems of PR which would both reflect and restrain these changes in society (Rokkan, 1970). More recent transitions have underlined this "rational actor" model of electoral system choice. Thus, threatened incumbent regimes in Ukraine and Chile adopted systems which they thought would maximize their electoral prospects: a two-round runoff system which overrepresents the former Communists in the Ukraine (Birch, 1997), and a unusual form of PR in two-member districts which was calculated to over-represent the second-place party in Chile (Barczak, 1997). An interesting exception which proves the validity of this rule was the ANC's support for a PR system for South Africa's first postapartheid elections. Retention of the existing FPTP system would almost undoubtedly have seen the overrepresentation of the ANC, as the most popular party, but it would also have led to problems of minority exclusion and uncertainty. The ANC made a rational decision that their long-term interest would be better served by a system which enabled them to control their nominated candidates and bring possibly destabilizing electoral elements "into the tent" rather than giving them a reason to attack the system itself.

Lastly, the efficacy of electoral system design needs to be seen in juxtaposition to the broader constitutional framework of the state. This paper concentrates on elections that constitute legislatures. The impact of the electoral system on the membership and dynamics of that body will always be significant, but the electoral system's impact upon political accommodation and democratization more generally is tied to the amount of power held by the legislature and that body's relationship to other political institutions. The importance of electoral system engineering is heightened in centralized, unicameral parliamentary systems, and is maximized when the legislature is then constitutionally obliged to produce an oversize executive cabinet of national unity drawn from all significant parties that gain parliamentary representation.

Similarly, the efficacy of electoral system design is incrementally diminished as power is eroded away from the parliament. Thus, constitutional structures which diffuse and separate powers will distract attention from elections to the legislature and will require the constitutional designer to focus on the interrelationships between executives and legislatures, between upper and lower houses of parliament, and between national and regional and local government. This is not to diminish the importance of electoral systems for these other institutions (for example, presidencies or federal legislatures); rather, it highlights the fact that constitutional engineering becomes increasingly complex as power is devolved away from the center. Each of the following institutional components of the state may fragment the focal points of political power and thus diminish the significance of electoral system design on the overall political climate: (1) a directly elected president, (2) a bicameral parliament with a balance of power between the two houses, (3) a degree of federalism and/or regional asymmetrical arrangements. Similarly, greater centralization of power in the hands of one figure, such as a president, raises the electoral stakes. Thus some analysts have attributed the failure of democracy in Angola in 1992 to the combination of a strong presidential system with a run-off electoral system, which pitted the leaders of two competing armed factions in a head-to-head struggle that only one could win, thus almost guaranteeing that the "loser" would resume hostilities (Reid, 1993).

THE WORLD OF ELECTORAL SYSTEMS

There are countless electoral system variations, but essentially they can be split into 11 main systems which fall into three broad families. The most common way to look at electoral systems is to group them by how closely they translate national votes won into parliamentary seats won; that is, how *proportional* they are. To do this, one needs to look at both the vote-seat relationship and the level of wasted votes.[14] If we take the proportionality principle into account, along with some other considerations such as how many members are elected from each district and how many votes the elector has, we are left with the family structure illustrated in Figure 1.

Plurality-Majority Systems

These comprise three plurality systems—first past the post, the block vote, and the party block vote—and two majority systems, the alternative vote and the two-round system.

1. *First-Past-the-Post (FPTP)* is the world's most commonly used system. Contests are held in single-member districts, and the winner is the candidate with the most votes, but not necessarily an absolute majority of the votes. FPTP is supported primarily on the grounds of simplicity, and its tendency to produce representatives beholden to defined geographic areas. Countries that use this system include the United Kingdom, the United States, India, Canada, and most countries that were once part of the British Empire.

2. The *Block Vote (BV)* is the application of FPTP in multi- rather than single-member districts. Voters have as many votes as there are seats to be filled, and the highest-polling candidates fill the positions regardless of the percentage of the vote they actually achieve. This system is used in some parts of Asia and the Middle East.

3. The *Party Block Vote (PBV)* operates in multimember districts, and requires voters to choose between party lists of candidates rather than individuals. The party which wins most votes takes all the seats in the district, and its entire list of candidates is duly elected. Variations on this system can be used to balance ethnic representation, as is the case in Singapore (discussed in more detail later).

4. Under the *Alternative Vote (AV)* system, electors rank the candidates in order of choice, marking a "1" for their favorite candidate, "2" for their second choice, "3" for their third choice, and so on. The system thus enables voters to express their preferences between candidates, rather than simply their first choice. If no candidate has over 50 percent of first preferences, lower order preference votes are transferred until a majority winner emerges. This system is used in Australia and some other South Pacific countries.

5. The *Two-Round System (TRS)* has two rounds of voting, often a week or a fortnight apart. The first round is the same as a normal FPTP election. If a candidate receives an absolute majority of the vote, then he or she is elected outright, with no need for a second ballot. If, however, no

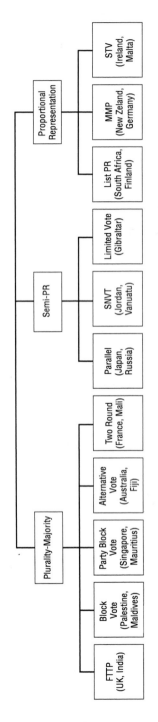

FIGURE 1. The world of electoral systems.

candidate has received an absolute majority, then a second round of voting is conducted, and the winner of this round is declared elected. This system is widely used in France, former French colonies, and some parts of the former Soviet Union.

Semi-Proportional Systems

Semi-PR systems are those which inherently translate votes cast into seats won in a way that falls somewhere in between the proportionality of PR systems and the majoritarianism of plurality-majority systems. The three semi-PR electoral systems used for legislative elections are the single nontransferable vote (SNTV), parallel (or mixed) systems, and the limited vote (LV).

6. In *SNTV Systems*, each elector has one vote but there are several seats in the district to be filled, and the candidates with the highest number of votes fill these positions. This means that in a four-member district, for example, one would on average need only just over 20 percent of the vote to be elected. This system is used today only in Jordan and Vanuatu, but is most often associated with Japan, which used SNTV until 1993.

7. *Parallel Systems* use both PR lists and single-member districts running side by side (hence the term parallel). Part of the parliament is elected by proportional representation, part by some type of plurality or majority method. Parallel systems have been widely adopted by new democracies in the 1990s, perhaps because, on the face of it, they appear to combine the benefits of PR lists with single-member district representation. Today, parallel systems are used in Russia, Japan, South Korea, Thailand and the Philippines, among others.

8. The *Limited Vote (LV)*, used in Gibraltar, the Spanish upper house, and in many U.S. local government elections, usually gives voters one fewer vote than there are seats to be filled. In its Spanish and U.K. manifestations, the limited vote shared many of the properties of the block vote, but Lijphart, Pintor, and Stone (1986) argue that because it facilities minority representation it should be referred to as a semiproportional system.

Proportional Representation Systems

All proportional representation (PR) systems aim to reduce the disparity between a party's share of national votes and its share of parliamentary seats. For example, if a major party wins 40 percent of the votes, it should also win around 40 percent of the seats, and a minor party with 10 percent of the votes should similarly gain 10 percent of the seats. For many new democracies, particularly those that face deep divisions, the inclusion of all significant groups in the parliament can be an important condition for democratic consolidation. Outcomes based on consensus-building and power-sharing usually include a PR system.

Criticisms of PR are twofold: that it gives rise to coalition governments, with disadvantages such as party system fragmentation and government instability; and that PR produces a weak linkage between a representative and her or his geographical electorate. And since voters are expected to vote for parties rather than individuals or groups of individuals, it is a difficult system to operate in societies that have embryonic or loose party structures.

9. *List PR Systems* are the most common type of PR. Most forms of list PR are held in large, multimember districts that maximize proportionality. List PR requires each party to present a list of candidates to the electorate. Electors vote for a party rather than a candidate, and parties receive seats in proportion to their overall share of the national vote. Winning candidates are taken from the lists in order of their respective position. This system is widely used in continental Europe, Latin America, and southern Africa.

10. *Mixed Member Proportional* (MMP) *Systems,* as used in Germany, New Zealand, Bolivia, Italy, Mexico, Venezuela, and Hungary, attempt to combine the positive attributes of both majoritarian and PR electoral systems. A proportion of the parliament (roughly half in the cases of Germany, New Zealand, Bolivia, and Venezuela) is elected by plurality-majority methods, usually from single-member districts, while the remainder is constituted by PR lists. The PR seats are used to compensate for any disproportionality produced by the district seat results. Single-member districts also ensure that voters have some geographical representation.

11. The *Single Transferable Vote* (STV) uses multimember districts, where voters rank candidates in order of preference on the ballot paper in the same manner as AV. After the total number of first-preference votes are tallied, a "quota" of votes is established, which a candidate must achieve to be elected. Any candidate who has more first preferences than the quota is immediately elected. If no one has achieved the quota, the candidate with the lowest number of first preferences is eliminated, and their second preferences are redistributed among remaining candidates. And the surplus votes of elected candidates (i.e., those votes above the quota) are redistributed according to the second preferences on the ballot papers until all seats for the constituency are filled. This system is well established in Ireland and Malta.

THE IMPORTANCE OF THE PROCESS WHICH LED TO THE CHOICE OF ELECTORAL SYSTEM

Although the choice of electoral system is one of the most important institutional decisions for any democracy, it is relatively unusual in historical terms for electoral systems to be consciously and deliberately chosen. Often, the choice of electoral system is essentially accidental: the result of an unusual combination of circumstances, of a passing trend, or of a quirk of history. The impacts of colonialism and the effects of influential neighbors are often especially strong. Yet in almost all cases, a particular electoral system choice has a profound effect on the future political life of the country concerned. Electoral systems, once chosen, tend to remain fairly constant, as political interests quickly congeal around and respond to the incentives for election presented by the system.

If it is rare that electoral systems are deliberately chosen, it is rarer still that they are carefully designed for the particular historical and social conditions present in a given country. This is particularly the case for new democracies. Any new democracy must choose (or inherit) an electoral system to elect its parliament. But such decisions are often taken within one of two circumstances. Either political actors lack basic knowledge and information, and the choices and consequences of different electoral systems are not fully recognized or, conversely, political actors do have knowledge of electoral system consequences and thus promote designs which they perceive will maximize their own advantage (see Taagepera, 1998). In both of these scenarios, the choices that are made are sometimes not the best ones for the long-term political health of the country concerned; at times, they can have disastrous consequences for a country's democratic prospects.

The way in which an electoral system is chosen can thus be as important and enlightening as the choice itself. There are four ways in which most electoral systems are adopted: via colonial inheritance, through conscious design, by external imposition, and by accident. We will now deal with each of these processes in turn.

Colonial Inheritance

Inheriting an electoral system from colonial times is perhaps the most common way through which democratizing societies come to use a particular electoral system. For example, out of 53 former British colonies and members of the Commonwealth of Nations, a full 37 (or 70 percent) use classic first-past-the-post systems inherited from Westminster. Eleven of the 27 Francophone territories use the French two-round system, while the majority of the remaining 16 countries use list PR, a system used by the French on and off since 1945 for parliamentary elections, and widely for municipal elections. Fifteen out of the 17 Spanish-speaking countries and territories use PR (as does Spain), while Guatemala and Ecuador use list PR as part of their parallel systems. Finally, all six Lusophone countries use list PR, as in Portugal. This pattern even extends to the former Soviet Republics of the Commonwealth of Independent States (CIS): eight of these states use the two-round system in some form (see Reynolds and Reilly, 1997).

Colonial inheritance of an electoral system is perhaps the *least* likely way to ensure that the institution is appropriate to a country's needs, as the begetting colonial power was usually very different socially and culturally from the society colonized. And even where the colonizer sought to stamp much of its political ethos on the occupied land, it rarely succeeded in obliterating indigenous power relations and traditional modes of political discourse. It is therefore not surprising that the colonial inheritance of Westminster systems has been cited as an impediment to stability in a number of developing countries, e.g., in the Caribbean (Lewis, 1965), Nigeria (see Diamond, 1995, and Laitin, 1986) and Malawi (see Reynolds, 1995). Similarly, Mali's use of the French two-round system has been questioned by Vengroff (1994), Indonesia's Dutch-inherited list PR system has been cited as restricting that country's political development (MacBeth, 1998), and Jordan and Palestine's use of the British-inspired block vote has also led to problems (Reynolds and Elklit, 1997).

Conscious Design

The deliberate design of electoral systems to achieve certain preconceived outcomes is not a new phenomenon, although its incidence has waxed and waned over this century. Enthusiasm for electoral engineering appears to correspond, logically enough, to successive "waves" of democratization (Huntington, 1991). Huntington's first wave, from 1828 until 1926, saw several examples of deliberate electoral engineering that are now well-established electoral institutions. The alternative vote system introduced for federal elections in Australia in 1918, for example, was intended to mitigate the problems of conservative forces "splitting" their vote in the face of a rising Labor Party. It did exactly that (Reilly, 1997b). At Irish independence in 1922, both the indigenous political elite and the departing British favored the single transferable vote due to its inherent fairness and protection of Protestant and Unionist minorities (Gallagher, 1997). The adoption of list PR systems in continental Europe occurred first in the most culturally diverse societies, such as Belgium and Switzerland, as a means of ensuring balanced inter-ethnic representation (Rokkan, 1970). All of these cases represented examples of conscious institutional engineering utilizing what were, at the time, new electoral systems in fledgling and divided democracies.

The short second wave of democratization in the decolonization decades after the second world war also saw the electoral system used as a lever for influencing the future politics of new democracies. Most of the second wave, however, featured less in the way of deliberate design and more in the way of colonial transfer. Thus, ethnically plural states in Africa and fragile independent nations in Asia inherited British first-past-the-post or French two-round systems; and in nearly all cases these inappropriate models, transplanted directly from colonial Western powers, contributed to an early "reverse wave" of democracy.

The "third wave" of democracy has seen a new appreciation of the necessity for and utility of well-crafted electoral systems as a key constitutional choice for new democracies. In recent years, transitions to democracy in Hungary, Bolivia, South Africa, Korea, Taiwan, Fiji, and elsewhere have all been accompanied by extensive discussion and debate about the merits of particular electoral system designs. A parallel process has taken place in established democracies, with Italy, Japan, and New Zealand all changing their electoral systems in the 1990s. In most cases, these choices are based on negotiations between political elites, but in some countries (e.g., Italy and New Zealand) public plebiscites have been held to determine the voters' choice on this most fundamental of electoral questions.

External Imposition

A small number of electoral systems were more consciously designed and imposed on nation states by external powers. Two of the most vivid examples of this phenomenon occurred in West Germany after the second world war, and in Namibia in the late 1980s.

In post-war Germany, both the departing British forces and the German parties were anxious to introduce a system which would avoid the damaging party proliferation and destabilization of the Weimar years,[15] and to incorporate the Anglo tradition of constituency representation because of unease with the 1919-1933 closed list electoral system, which denied the voters a choice between candidates as well as parties (Farrell, 1997:87-88). During 1946, elections in the French and American zones of occupation were held under the previous Weimar electoral system. But in the British zone a compromise was adopted which allowed electors to vote for constituency members with a number of list PR seats reserved to compensate for any disproportionality that arose from the districts. Thus, the mixed-member proportional (MMP) system, which has since been emulated by a number of other countries, was born. This mixed system was adopted for all parliamentary elections in 1949, but it was not until

1953 that two separate votes were introduced, one for the constituency member, and another based on the Länder which ultimately determined the party composition of the Bundestag. The imposition of a 5 percent national threshold for party list representation helped focus the party system around three major groupings after 1949 (the Social Democrats, Christian Democrats, and Free Democrats), although in all 12 parties gained representation in those first post-war national elections.

The rationale for a national list PR system in Namibia came initially from the United Nations, who urged as early as 1982 that any future nonracial electoral system ensure that political parties managing to gain substantial support in the election be rewarded with fair representation. The option of discarding the incumbent first-past-the-post electoral system (the whites-only system operating in what was the colony of South-West Africa) and moving to PR was proposed by Pik Botha, then South African Foreign Minister. South Africa had previously, but unsuccessfully, pressed for separate voters' rolls (à la Zimbabwe 1980-1985), which would have ensured the overrepresentation of whites in the new Constituent Assembly. After expressions of unease that South Africa was promoting PR solely in order to fractionalize the Assembly, the UN Institute for Namibia advised all political parties interested in a stable independence government "to reject any PR system that tends to fractionalize party representation" (see Cliffe et al., 1994:116). But this advice remained unheeded, and the option of a threshold for representation (one of the chief mechanisms for reducing the number of parties in a list PR system) was never put forward by the UN or made an issue by any of the political parties. For the first elections in 1989, the South West African People's Organization (SWAPO) expressed a preference for keeping the single member district system, no doubt reasonably expecting (as the dominant party) to be advantaged by such winner-take-all constituencies. However, when the Constituent Assembly met for the first time in November 1989, and each parliamentary party presented their draft constitution, SWAPO gave in on the issue of PR—apparently as a concession to the minority parties for which they hoped to gain reciprocal concessions on matters of more importance.

Accidental Adoption/Evolution

Although this paper concentrates on the possibilities of deliberate "electoral engineering," it is worth remembering that most electoral systems are *not* deliberately chosen. Often, choices are made through a kaleidoscope of accidents and miscommunications leading to a multitude of unintended consequences.

Accidental choices are not necessarily poor ones; in fact, sometimes they can be surprisingly appropriate. One example of this was the highly ethnically fragmented democracy of Papua New Guinea, which inherited the Alternative Vote (see below) from its colonial master, Australia, for its first three elections in the 1960s and 1970s. Because this system required voters to list candidates preferentially on the ballot paper, elections encouraged a spectrum of alliances and vote trading between competing candidates and different communal groups, with candidates attempting to win not just first preferences but second and third preference votes as well. This led to cooperative campaigning tactics, moderate positions, and the early development of political parties. When this system was changed, political behavior become more exclusionary and less accommodatory, and the nascent party system quickly unraveled (Reilly, 1997a).

With the benefit of hindsight, Papua New Guinea thus appears to have been the fortuitous recipient of a possibly uniquely appropriate electoral system for its social structure. Most accidental or evolutionary choices are, however, more likely to lead to less fortuitous unintended consequences—particularly for the actors who designed them. For example, when Jordan reformed its electoral system in 1993, on the personal initiative of King Hussein, it had the effect of increasing minority representation but also facilitating the election of Islamic fundamentalists to the legislature (Reynolds and Elklit, 1997). Many fledgling democracies in the 1950s and 1960s adopted copies of the British system, despite consistent misgivings from Westminster that it was "of doubtful value as an export to tropical colonies, to primitive societies in Africa and to complex societies in India."[16] The sorry history of many such choices has underlined the importance of designing electoral and constitutional rules for the specific conditions of the country at hand, rather than blithely assuming that the same "off the shelf" constitutional design will work identically in different social, political and economic circumstances.

ELECTORAL SYSTEMS AND CONFLICT MANAGEMENT

The comparative experience suggests that four specific systems are particularly suitable for divided societies. These are usually recommended as part of overall constitutional engineering packages, in which the electoral system is one element. Some constitutional engineering packages emphasize inclusiveness and proportionality; others emphasize moderation and accommodation. The four major choices in this regard (1) *consociationalism* (based, in part, on list proportional representation); (2) *centripetalism* (based, in part, on the vote-pooling potential of the alternative vote); (3) *integrative consensualism* (based, in part, on the single transferable vote), and (4) a construct not previously mentioned, which we call *explicitism*, which explicitly recognizes communal groups and gives them institutional representation, which in theory can be based on almost any electoral system, but in practice is usually based on the block vote (e.g., in Mauritius, Lebanon and Singapore).

Consociationalism

One of the most discussed prescriptions for plural (segmented) societies remains that of *consociationalism*, a term first used by Althusius, and rescued from obscurity by Lijphart in the late 1960s. Consociationalism entails a power-sharing agreement within government, brokered between clearly defined segments of society which may be joined by citizenship but divided by ethnicity, religion, and language. Examples of consociational societies include Belgium, the Netherlands, Austria, and Switzerland. Cyprus and Lebanon are cited as countries which had, but no longer have, a consociational ethos (Lijphart, 1977). The mechanics of consociationalism can be distilled into four basic elements which must be present to make the constitution worthy of the consociational name. They are: (1) executive power sharing among the representatives of all significant groups (*a grand coalition in the cabinet*); (2) a high degree of internal autonomy for groups that wish to have it (*constitutionally entrenched segmental autonomy*); (3) proportional representation (through list PR) and proportional allocation of civil service positions and public funds (*proportionality*); and (4) a minority veto on the most vital issues (*a mutual veto for parties in the executive*) (Lijphart, 1977:25).

These arrangements encourage government to become an inclusive multiethnic coalition, in contrast to the adversarial nature of a Westminster winner-take-all democracy. Consociationalism rests on the premise that in bitterly divided societies the stakes are too high for politics to be conducted as a zero-sum game. Also, the risks of governmental collapse and state instability are too great for parties to view the executive branch of government as a prize to be won or lost. The fact that grand coalitions exist in Westminster democracies at times of particular crisis further supports the consociational claim.[17]

Arguments in Favor

Consociationalism is particularly reliant on a PR electoral system to provide a broadly representative legislature upon which the other tenets of minority security can be based. Lijphart clearly expresses a preference for using party list forms of PR rather than STV, or by implication open list PR systems and mixed systems which give the voter multiple votes. In a discussion of the proposals for South Africa he noted that STV might indeed be superior for reasonably homogeneous societies, but "for plural societies list PR is clearly the better method" because it, (1) allows for higher district magnitude—thus increasing proportionality, (2) is less vulnerable to gerrymandering, and (3) is simpler (than STV) for the voters and vote counters and thus will be less open to suspicion.[18]

In many respects, the strongest arguments for PR derive from the way in which the system avoids the anomalous results of plurality-majority systems and facilitates a more representative legislature. For many new democracies, particularly those which face deep societal divisions, the inclusion of all significant groups in the parliament can be a near-essential condition for democratic consolidation. Failing to ensure that both minorities and majorities have a stake in these nascent political systems can have catastrophic consequences. Recent transitional elections in Chile (1989), Namibia (1989), Nicaragua (1990), Cambodia (1993), South Africa (1994), Mozambique (1994), and Bosnia (1996) all used a form of regional or national list PR for their founding elections, and some scholars have identified the choice of a proportional rather than a majoritarian system as being a key component of their successful transitions to democracy (Lijphart ,1977; Reynolds, 1995). By bringing minorities into the process and fairly representing all significant political parties in the new legislature, regardless of the extent or distribution of their support base, PR has been seen as being an integral element of creating an inclusive and legitimate postauthoritarian regime.

More specifically, PR systems in general are praised because of the way in which they: (1) Faithfully translate votes cast into seats won, and thus avoid some of the more destabilizing and "unfair" results thrown up by plurality-majority electoral systems; (2) give rise to very few wasted votes; (3) facilitate minority parties' access to representation; (4) encourage parties to present inclusive and socially diverse lists of candidates; (5) make it more likely that the representatives of minority cultures/groups are elected;[19] (6) make it more likely that women are elected;[20] (7) restrict the growth of "regional fiefdoms";[21] and (8) make power-sharing between parties and interest groups more visible.

Arguments Against

While large-scale PR appears to be an effective instrument for smoothing the path of democratic transition, it may be less effective at promoting democratic *consolidation*. Developing countries in particular which have made the transition to democracy under list PR rules have increasingly found that the large, multimember districts required to achieve proportional results also create considerable difficulties in terms of political accountability and responsiveness between elected politicians and voters. Democratic consolidation requires the establishment of a meaningful relationship between the citizen and the state, and many new democracies—particularly those in agrarian societies (Barkan, 1995)—have much higher demands for constituency service at the local level than they do for representation of all shades of ideological opinion in the legislature. It is therefore increasingly being argued in South Africa, Indonesia, Cambodia, and elsewhere that the choice of a permanent electoral system should encourage a high degree of *geographic accountability*, by having members of parliament who represent small, territorially defined districts and servicing the needs of their constituency, in order to establish a meaningful relationship between the rulers and the ruled. While this does not preclude all PR systems—there are a number of ways of combining single-member districts with proportional outcomes—it does rule out the national list PR systems often favored by consociationalists.

In terms of electoral system choice, the major critique of list PR systems is thus that they fail to provide any link between a member and his or her electorate, hence lessening the "geographic accountability" between the two. But there are other critiques of list PR in divided societies that center on the ease with which ethnic leaders can be elected exclusively by members of their own group, thus replicating (rather than breaking down) social divisions in the legislature. The experience of list PR in post-Dayton Bosnia is a good example of how proportionality alone will not encourage accommodation. In Bosnia, groups are represented in parliament in proportion to their numbers in the community as a whole, but because parties can rely exclusively on the votes of members of their own community for their electoral success, there is little incentive for them to behave accommodatively on ethnic issues. In fact, the incentives work in the other direction. As it is easy to mobilize support by playing the "ethnic card," major parties in Bosnia have every incentive to emphasize ethnic issues and sectarian appeals. Bosnia's 1996 elections were effectively an ethnic census, with electors voting along ethnic lines and each of the major nationalist parties gaining support almost exclusively from their own ethnic group (see Reilly, 1998b).

More generally, consociationalism rests on several key assumptions that may not always be viable in divided societies. The most important of these is the assumption that ethnic leaders will be more moderate on key sectarian issues than their supporters. While this may hold true in some cases, it appears to be untrue as a generalized proposition about the relationship between ethnic elites and policy positions on ethnic issues. In fact, some studies have argued the opposite: leaderships of ethnic parties are often the ones who have the most to gain by maintaining ethnocentric politics.[22] Furthermore, the ability of leaders to compromise on issues may be extremely limited: "it has been shown repeatedly that leadership leeway is very narrow on issues of ethnic power in severely divided societies. Compromisers can readily be replaced by extremists on their flank" (Horowitz, 1997:439). The lack of a mechanism to encourage accommodation means that consociational prescriptions rely, sometimes unwisely, on enlightened political leadership and preparedness to compromise to achieve accommodatory outcomes.

Conclusion

The underlying ethos of consociationalism stresses that while there is joint decision making over common interests, regarding a cultural minority's area of exclusive domain the minority should be autonomous. This requires a clear definition of groups and group rights, which has led to the criticism that consociationalism may well perpetuate divisions rather than alleviate them. Indeed, Lijphart argues that "it is in the nature of consociational democracy, at least initially, to make plural societies more thoroughly plural. Its approach is not to abolish or weaken segmental cleavages but to recognize them explicitly and to turn the segments into constructive elements of a stable democracy" (1977:42).

Consociationalism is probably best seen as a stop-gap measure, the lesser of two evils which keeps the lid on the pressure cooker of a divided society that is about to blow and perhaps manages to turn down the heat just a little. Perhaps the most powerful criticism is that, by entrenching segments and defining all politics in those divisive terms, one actually postpones or even obstructs the breakdown of segmental barriers.[23] Indeed, some of the favorable conditions that Lijphart quotes for consociationalism seem to guard against it withering away. The way in which power-sharing requires geographically concentrated groups who have autonomy, not only in regional affairs, may ultimately increase the segmental divides. The tension remains: How does one recognize segmental groups, while at the same time attempt to diminish their importance? An even greater danger exists of imposing *ethnically aware* consociational structures on societies where political segments are not clearly or primarily defined along the lines of ethnicity. Nagata argues that in some cases, "the depth of segmental cleavages frequently follows rather than precedes consociational arrangements, thus creating instead of solving problems of pluralism" (1979:506).

The great value of consociationalism is that it offers powerful conflict-resolving solutions to those divided societies which show no hope of generating such interethnic political accommodation. It is the solution when all else fails. But if consociational structures are entrenched in plural societies which do show potential for the withering away of ethnic voting, then the very institutions designed to alleviate tensions may merely entrench the perception that all politics must be ethnic politics.

Consociationalism provides few incentives for political entrepreneurs to appeal for support beyond their own ethnic bases.

Centripetalism

An alternative electoral path to accommodation in deeply divided societies is what we (following Sisk, 1995) call "centripetalism": institutions and policies which encourage cooperation and centrist policies, and which counter extremism and conflict behavior. Centripetalism focuses on the electoral system as the chief agent of interethnic accommodation because of the incentives for election that such systems provide. Centripetalists argue that the use of particular electoral rules which encourage politicians to campaign for the votes of members of rival groups, via "vote-pooling" and "preference swapping" can induce interethnic bargaining and promote accommodative behavior. At the core of this approach, as developed by Donald Horowitz (1985, 1990, 1991), is the need "to make politicians reciprocally dependent on the votes of members of groups other than their own."[24]

The most reliable way of achieving this aim, according to proponents of the centripetal approach, is to offer sufficient electoral incentives for campaigning politicians to court voter support from other groups. In deeply divided societies, this can be very difficult to achieve. Under conditions of purely ascriptive ethnic identity and hostility, for example, almost nothing will convince a member of one ethnic group to cast his or her vote for a member of a rival group. However, some electoral systems such as the alternative vote (AV) permit (or even require) voters to declare not only their first choice of candidate on a ballot, but also their second, third, and subsequent choices amongst all candidates standing. This feature presents candidates who wish to maximize their electoral prospects with a strong incentive to try and attract the second preferences of voters from other groups (the assumption being that the first choice of voters will usually be a candidate from their own group). An alternative strategy is for major parties contesting FPTP elections in heterogeneous districts to nominate members of different ethnic groups as their chosen candidates in different districts. In Malaysia, for example, Chinese voters will help elect Muslim candidates in some seats, while Muslims will help elect Chinese in others.

Arguments in Favor

The argument for the integrative effects of AV is premised on the assumption that politicians are rational actors who will do what needs to be done to gain election. Under AV, "what needs to be done" varies considerably depending on the makeup of the electorate. The optimal scenario is a case where no candidate can be assured of an outright majority of support, so that the role of second and later preferences becomes crucial to attracting an overall majority. Those candidates who successfully "pool" both their own first preferences and the second preferences of others will be more successful than those who fail to attract any second-order support. To attract such second-order support, candidates need to attract the support of groups other than their own, and this is usually achieved by their moving to the center on policy issues to attract floating voters, or by successfully accommodating "fringe" issues into their broader policy. There is a long history of both these types of behavior in Australian elections, the only established democracy to use AV. There is also widespread agreement that AV has facilitated coalition arrangements in Australia, such as that between the Liberal and National parties, and that it works to the advantage of center candidates and parties, encouraging moderate policy positions and a search for the "middle ground" (see Reilly, 1997b).

In cases of deeply divided societies, however, policy-based cleavages are usually considerably less salient than ethnic or linguistic identities. But the incentives for election under AV rules can still operate in the same manner: candidates will do what they need to do to gain election. Where a candidate needs the support of other ethnic groups to gain election, there is a powerful incentive for him or her to reach out to these groups in search of their second preferences. The more groups present in a given constituency, the more likely it is that meaningful vote pooling will take place. To build support from other groups, candidates must behave moderately and accommodatively towards them. In ethnically divided societies, this means that electoral incentives can promote policy concessions: even small minorities have a value in terms of where their preferences are directed, as small numbers of votes could always be the difference between victory and defeat for major candidates.

The only time that these theories have been properly tested has been in preindependence Papua New Guinea (PNG), which held elections in 1964, 1968, and 1972 under AV rules. Analysis of the relationship in PNG between political behavior and the electoral system provides significant evidence that accommodative vote-pooling behavior *was* encouraged by the incentives presented by AV, and further significant evidence that behavior became markedly less accommodative when AV was replaced by FPTP, under which the incentives for electoral victory are markedly different. Under AV, vote pooling took place in three primary ways, all of which were predicated on the assumption that most voters would invariably give their first preference to their own clan or "home" candidate. The most common and successful method of vote pooling was for a candidate who had a limited "home" support base to campaign widely for second-level support among rival groups. This required a range of techniques, such as translating campaign speeches and traveling widely throughout an electorate, with the essential request being not for a first-preference vote but for a second preference. This enabled electors to cast their primary vote for their ascriptive candidate—an essential element in cases of ascriptive ethnic identity—but also to indicate their second choice if their ascriptive candidate was not elected. For this strategy to succeed, candidates needed to be able to sell themselves as the "second-best" choice, which meant, in general, someone who would look after all groups, not just his own. A second strategy for victory under AV was for candidates with significant existing support bases to reach out to selected allies for secondary support. Traditional tribal contacts and allegiances, for example, could be utilized to create majority victors. This similarly necessitated a commitment to behave positively toward that group if elected. In one seat at the 1972 elections, for example, tribal leaders of previously hostile groups made deals with each other for preference support. The winning candidate forged particularly close connections with a traditional ally tribe via "intensive ties of ceremonial exchange," had urged his supporters to cast their preferences for a member of a hostile rival tribe as well as for himself, and consequently received a generous proportion of that opponent's second preferences to win the seat. A third strategy, increasingly common by the time of the third AV election in 1972, was for groups and candidates to form mutual alliances, sometimes campaigning together and urging voters to cast reciprocal preferences for one or the other. This similarly necessitated a strong cooperative approach to electoral competition (Reilly, 1998a).

The central appeal of the integrated approach is thus that it produces *incentives* for accommodative behavior—via the search for secondary support—rather than relying on *constraints* (such as minority vetoes) against hostility. A second virtue is that it relies on popular rather than elite activity: campaigning politicians and their supporters are directly rewarded by moderation and can directly expect to reap what they sow. Candidates who are elected will be dependent on the votes of groups other than their own for their parliamentary positions, and can be expected to serve the needs of these groups as well as their own ethnic group if they are to establish their positions and gain reelection. A system similar to AV has been used to elect the Sri Lankan President since 1978, and some observers have argued that this has led to increasing recognition of minority Tamil and Muslim interests by the major Sinhalese parties (de Silva, 1994; Reilly, 1997b). AV was also recommended for elections to postapartheid South Africa (Horowitz, 1991) and was recently chosen as the basis of a new, nonracial constitution in Fiji as the best way of encouraging the development of peaceful multiethnic politics in that deeply divided society (Constitution Review Commission, 1996). Other arguments for AV include its use of small single-member electorates, thus guaranteeing geographic accountability, and the fact that it guarantees that victorious candidates will be supported by an absolute majority of the electorate.

Arguments Against

Critics of the centripetal approach have focused on four themes. The first is that there are no examples of successful centripetalism in practice (Sisk, 1996; Lijphart, 1995a), and that "although vote pooling is theoretically compelling, there is simply insufficient empirical evidence at the level of national politics to support claims that subsequent preference voting can lead to accommodative outcomes."[25] In fact, there is a considerable range of evidence from PNG, Australia, Sri Lanka, and elsewhere which demonstrates centripetalism in action, although much of this material remains relatively obscure (see Reilly, 1998a). Other objections to AV are more substantial. The first is that, because AV is a majoritarian system, it results in highly disproportional electoral results and minority exclusion, especially when compared to PR systems (Lijphart, 1991; Reynolds, 1995). There is some truth in this, although many of these arguments focus less on standard single-member AV than on the multimember AV system proposed by Horowitz (1991), which did indeed produce dangerously disproportional results when used in the Australian Senate between the wars (Reilly and Maley, 1999; Lijphart, 1997). Research indicates that single-member AV is actually among the *least* disproportional of majoritarian systems, although it is clearly less proportional than PR systems (Reilly, 1997a; but see Lijphart, 1997, for a reply). A second criticism argues that AV actually acts in practice much like other majoritarian electoral systems such as TRS and FPTP, and consequently that there is no more incentive to compromise under AV than under these systems (Lijphart, 1991). Again, the evidence from PNG in particular tends to undermine this argument, as the political behavior at both the elite and mass level became markedly less accommodatory when the electoral system changed from AV to FPTP (Reilly, 1997a).

The third criticism is that AV would fail to encourage integrative behavior in some regions because of the demographic distribution of ethnic groups (Reynolds, 1995). This last criticism is the most significant. In many ethnically divided countries, members of the same ethnic group tend to cluster together, which means that the relatively small, single-member districts which are a feature of AV would, in these cases, result in constituencies which are ethnically homogeneous rather than heteroge-

neous. Where one candidate is confident of achieving an absolute majority of first preferences due to the domination of his or her own ethnic
group in an area, they need only focus on maximizing their own vote
share from their own supporters in order to win the seat. This means that
the "vote-pooling" between different ethnic groups which is a precondition for the accommodative influences of AV would not, in fact, occur.
Most regions of Latin America and southern Africa, for example, feature
geographically concentrated ethnic groups.[26] For this reason, it is likely
that AV will work best either in cases of extreme ethnic fragmentation
(such as that found in some areas of the South Pacific and Central Africa)
or, alternatively, the more common scenario of a few large ethnic groups
which are widely dispersed and intermixed (e.g., Malaysia, Lebanon,
Singapore, Fiji, Mauritius, Trinidad and Tobago, etc.). Both of these social
structures, which appear to be particularly common in the Asia-Pacific
region, would result in ethnically heterogeneous electoral districts and
thus, under AV rules, strong incentives towards accommodative prefer-
ence-swapping deals (see Reilly, 1998a).

Conclusion

The arguments for and against centripetalism are a good example of
the contextual nature of electoral system design, and how proponents of
different approaches run the risk of talking past each other. There is strong
evidence that AV has worked or will work well in some types of social
setting (PNG, Fiji, and other intermixed areas) but poorly in some others
(e.g., ethnically concentrated states in southern Africa). AV also requires a
reasonable degree of literacy to be utilized effectively, and because it
operates in single-member districts it can often produce results that are
disproportional when compared to PR systems. These are drawbacks, but
they are mitigated by the strength of incentives towards centripetal politics that AV appears to encourage. The experience of AV in PNG, Sri
Lanka, and in Australia all suggests that it does encourage moderate,
centrist politics and enables diverse interests to be aggregated. In the
right type of social setting, it can provide significant incentives for
accommodatory and cooperative politics, and deserves more consideration as an attractive model of electoral system design, particularly for
ethnically intermixed states, than it has received to date.

Integrative Consensualism

In many ways the theory of *integrative consensualism* (as advocated by
Reynolds, 1996) attempts to build on the philosophies underpinning both
consociationalism and centripetalism, by retaining the key consociational

planks of mandatory executive power sharing and a PR electoral system, but utilizing the centripetal electoral system incentives of STV rather than rigid list PR. Indeed, one of the two most important institutional planks of integrative consensualism is the STV electoral system (the other being the rejection of institutions which entrench ethnic or cultural political blocks within the party system).

There are important differences, both theoretically and practically, between consociationalism and an integrative consensualism. Both types contain power-sharing provisions but are based upon different structures, objectives and, most importantly, rest on different premises. As noted earlier, consociationalism rests on the premise that society is deeply divided along ethnic lines, what Robert Price calls "politicized ethnicity," segmented into a number of nonconversing and antagonistic cultural groups (Price, 1995). Voting affiliation is primarily driven by such ascriptive identities. While there are strong arguments in favor of consociationalism for ethnically polarized societies, other types of societies may be able to manage sociopolitical conflicts with consensus-oriented systems in which some of the institutional mechanisms of consociation are practiced, but not all of them are institutionalized. Such consensus systems rest on the premise that society is conflictual and may indeed be divided, but those divisions and voting behavior are not primarily motivated by ascriptive identities. Other cleavages, along the lines of class, wealth, regionalism, and clan, may be more salient.

Arguments in Favor

Institutionally, *integrative consensus* democracy prescribes STV in order to encourage cross-cutting ethnic cleavages, while at the same time ensuring the fair representation and inclusion of minorities in decision making. The argument is that if the institutional incentives embedded within integrative consensual democracy work as hypothesized, they will allow the space for and, indeed, provide incentives for, the growth of multiethnic political parties; but, they will not guarantee that such parties flourish. It follows, therefore, that integrative consensus democracy is only an option in plural societies which show signs that ethnicity need not endure as the sole driving force of politics. If voters are never likely to look outside of their ascriptive identity to vote for nonethnic parties, then elections will never be anything more than *ethnic* or *racial censuses*, and integrative consensualism is redundant. In a society where politics is determined entirely by primordial affiliations, consociationalism may be the only viable option.

Interestingly, the rationale of integrative consensus shares much with the logic of centripetalism, but its institutional prescriptions are at variance with those prescribed by Horowitz and Reilly and are likely to produce different results. Chiefly, integrative consensualism rests on the principles of proportionality and coalition government, while it is more likely that elections under centripetalism would produce nonproportional parliaments and single-party executives. Reynolds argues that, in a plural society which is ripe for consensus government, members of an ethnic group may indeed be more likely to vote for a certain political party, but it is not clear that they do so out of a knee-jerk desire to vote as a communal block for candidates of a similar skin color. Where there is doubt about what drives voting behavior, and the intuition that the electorate is more sophisticated than an ethnic census explanation would give them credit for, then there is space for constitutional mechanisms which encourage crosscutting cleavages. The goal of integrative consensus strategies is to proliferate such incentives, while at the same time retaining the benefits of inclusionary government (i.e., proportional representation through STV, grand coalition cabinets, and a variety of access points to political power).

While the consociational and integrative consensus types share a number of traits (indeed they are both forms of power-sharing or consensual democracy), such as proportionality, federalism, bicameralism, and minority vetoes, they differ in the institutional mechanisms they utilize to facilitate such traits. One of the key differences is the choice of electoral system. While consociationalism is nearly always based on a list PR system, integrative consensualism requires the use of the single transferable vote to encourage party appeals beyond defined ethnic boundaries. Under this system, segments of opinion would be represented proportionately in the legislature, but there would be a great incentive for political elites to appeal to the members of other segments, given that second preferences on the ballot paper are of prime importance. Lakeman argues that under STV "political considerations can gradually assume more importance and racial ones less, without the elector ever being faced with a conflict of loyalties" (1974:136).

Arguments Against

Advocates of majoritarianism see the dangers of immobilism and paralysis just as inherent in consensual government as in consociationalism (due to the mandated oversize coalition governments). Proponents of both consociationalism and centripetalism have also criticized consensualism's electoral recommendations. Lijphart argues that STV is better suited to homogenous societies than plural ones (Lijphart, 1990:11), while Horowitz objects to STV on the grounds that the threshold for winning a seat in a multimember STV district is too low to ensure that incentives for vote-pooling influence party campaign strategies (1991:191).

It is true that, with one important exception, the use of STV in divided societies to date has been limited, inconclusive, and generally not supportive of integral consensual theories. Until the 1998 "Good Friday" peace agreement in Northern Ireland, only two ethnically divided states had utilized STV in "one-off" national elections: Northern Ireland in 1973 (and again in 1982) and Estonia in 1990. In both cases, little vote-pooling took place. In elections to the abortive Northern Ireland Assembly, parties neither campaigned for nor received votes across the Protestant-Catholic divide, in part "because the chances of winning an extra seat by adding a few votes from the other community were much less than the chances of losing votes by appearing 'soft' on key sectarian issues."[27] In Estonia, which is similarly divided between the majority indigenous Estonian (60 percent) community and a minority (35 percent) immigrant Russian one, STV was used for the first national independence elections in 1990 before being replaced with list PR. Again, ethnicity appeared to be the dominant factor in voter choice at these elections, with little evidence of cross-ethnic voting.[28]

Conclusion

Just as there are few cases of the use of STV in divided societies, to date there have been no full-blown examples of the integrative typology in the real world. Perhaps the bundle of constitutional arrangements which come closest to the typology are the newly constructed arrangements for self-government and multistate consultation in Northern Ireland that were adopted and passed by referendum (in both the North and South) in May 1998. The Northern Irish Assembly elected in July 1998 consists of 108 parliamentarians elected by STV in 17 multimember districts. The size of the constituencies, already small in population, mean that a candidate will only need 2,000-3,000 votes to be elected. Other integrative consensus arrangements include obligatory power-sharing in the executive (the first prime minister will come from the largest community, while the deputy will come from the minority community), proportional power-sharing at all levels of government and in the special commissions set up to deal with particularly culturally contentious issues, and a minority veto over legislation deemed to be relevant to communal interests. However, these institutional mechanisms owe just as much to the theory of consociationalism and the designation of ethnic groups. Voters will self-identify themselves as Catholic/Nationalist or Protestant/Unionist, and offices will be shared upon that basis rather than simple party strength. Therefore, while the Northern Irish peace agreement instituted (or reinstituted) an electoral system aimed to encourage the development of cross-cutting ethnic voting behavior (as integrative consensus democracy would applaud), it mitigated these benefits by entrenching the single aspect of consociationalism which most solidifies ethnic identification (i.e., rewards, the trappings and offices of power, are allocated on the basis of groups rather than party strength per se).

Explicit Recognition of Communal Groups

A final approach to elections and conflict is to recognize explicitly the overwhelming importance of group identity in the political process, and to mandate this in the electoral law so that ethnic representation and the ratio of different ethnic groups in the legislature is fixed. There have been four distinct approaches which reflect this thinking: the use of communal electoral rolls; the presence of reserved seats for ethnic, linguistic, or other minorities; the use of ethnically mixed or mandated candidate lists; and the use of "best loser" seats to balance ethnic representation in the legislature. Each of these will be described below.

Communal Rolls

The most straightforward way of explicitly recognizing the importance of ethnicity is to utilize a system of communal representation. Seats are not only divided on a communal basis, but the entire system of parliamentary representation is similarly based on communal considerations. This usually means that each defined "community" has its own electoral roll and elects only members of its "own group" to Parliament.

Communal roll arrangements have often been used to cement a privileged position for certain minorities. Colonial India, for example, had separate electorates for Christians, Anglo-Saxons, Sikhs, and non-Brahmans. Burma's 1937 Constitution reserved 40 of the House of Representative's 132 seats for Karens, Indians, Chinese, Anglo-Indians, and Europeans. Rhodesia/Zimbabwe maintained separate electoral rolls for "white" electors until independence, and (as part of the constitutional settlement) for 7 years after. Cyprus continues to use communal roll arrangements to distinguish between Greek and Turkish communities, but the 24 seats set aside for Turkish Cypriots, who have boycotted Parliament since 1963, remain unfilled. But in most countries, most communal systems were abandoned after it became increasingly clear that communal electorates, while guaranteeing group representation, often had the perverse effect of undermining the path of accommodation between different groups as there were no incentives for political intermixing between communities. The issue of how to define a member of a particular group, and how to distribute electorates fairly between them, was also strewn with pitfalls.

Today, the only democracies which continue to use communal representation are Fiji and (for Maori only) New Zealand. Fiji has maintained a system of communal rolls for its indigenous, Indian, and "general" (i.e., European and Chinese) voters since independence in 1970. Until 1987, electors could vote not only for their own communal candidates but for some "national" candidates as well, a system known as "cross-voting." The military coup in 1987 led to the abolition of this provision and the entrenchment of an indigenous Fijian majority in the legislature. A constitutional review completed in 1996 recommended a "gradual but decisive" move away from communal politics toward genuine multiethnic competition (Constitution Review Commission, 1996). But the 1997 constitution, as enacted, did not make a decisive break with communalism, and two-thirds of all seats continue to be elected on a communal basis. Among established democracies, the one predominant example of a communal roll system left is the optional separate roll for Maori voters in New Zealand. Maori electors can choose to be on either the national electoral roll or a specific Maori roll, which elects five Maori MPs to Parliament. The results of New Zealand's first PR elections in 1996 could be said to have weakened the rationale for the communal system, however. Twice as many Maori MPs were elected from the general rolls as from the specific Maori roll.

Reserved Seats

Reserved seats are one way of ensuring the representation of specific minority groups in parliament. Countries as diverse as Jordan (Christians and Circassians), India (scheduled tribes and castes), Pakistan (non-Muslim minorities), Colombia ("black communities"), Croatia (Hungarian, Italian, Czech, Slovak, Ruthenian, Ukrainian, German and Austrian minorities), Slovenia (Hungarians and Italians), Taiwan (aboriginal community), Western Samoa (nonindigenous minorities), Niger (Tuareg), and the Palestinian Authority (Christians and Samaritans) reserve parliamentary seats for identifiable ethnic or religious minorities. Representatives from these reserved seats are usually elected in much the same manner as other members of parliament, but are often elected by members of the particular minority community designated in the electoral law.

Instead of formally reserved seats, regions can be overrepresented to facilitate the increased representation of minority groups. In essence this is the case in the United Kingdom, where Scotland and Wales have more MPs in the British House of Commons than they would be entitled to if population size were the only criteria. The same is true in the mountainous regions of Nepal. Electoral boundaries can also be manipulated to serve this purpose. The Voting Rights Act in the United States has in the past allowed the government to draw weird and wonderful districts with the sole purpose of creating majority Black, Latino, or Asian-American districts. This might be called "affirmative gerrymandering." While it is often deemed to be a normative good to represent small communities of interest, the manipulation of any electoral system to protect minority representation is rarely uncontroversial. It has often been argued that it is a better strategy to design structures which give rise to a representative parliament naturally rather than mandate the representation of members who may be viewed as "token" parliamentarians who have representation but often do not have genuine influence. Quota seats may also breed resentment on the behalf of majority populations and increase mistrust between various minority groups.

Ethnically Mixed Lists

Some countries use variations on a block vote to ensure balanced ethnic representation, as it enables parties to present ethnically diverse lists of candidates for election. In Lebanon, for example, election is dependent, at a practical level, on being part of a mixed list. In most cases, candidates must compete for election against other members of their own group. Electors choosing between party lists must thus make their choice on the basis of criteria other than ethnicity. In Singapore, most MPs are elected from multimember districts known as Group Representative Constituencies, which each return between three and six members from a single list of party or individual candidates. Of the candidates on each party or group list, at least one must be a member of the Malay, Indian, or some other minority community. Voters choose between these various lists of candidates with a single vote.

The advantages of such a system is that it is simple to use, encourages strong parties, and allows for parties to put up mixed slates of candidates in order to facilitate minority representation. However, a critical flaw is the production of "super-majoritarian" results, where one party can win almost all of the seats with a simple majority of the votes. In the Singaporean elections of 1991, for example, a 61 percent vote for the ruling People's Action Party gave it 95 percent of all seats in parliament, while in 1982 and 1995 the Mauritian elections saw a parliament with no opposition at all. To counter this possibility, the Lebanese constitution predetermines the ethnic composition of the entire parliament, and of key positions such as the president and the prime minister as well.

Best Loser

A final mechanism sometimes used in conjunction with the Block Vote is to assign seats to the "best loser" from a specified community. In Mauritius, for example, four "best loser" seats are allocated to the highest polling candidates of underrepresented ethnic groups in order to balance ethnic representation. Recently, however, there has been a strong movement in favor of the abolition of such seats, which are seen as representing the last vestiges of communalism in Mauritian politics (Mathur, 1997). Singapore also uses "best loser" seats for opposition candidates in some circumstances, as does Ecuador where, if the party which takes second-place wins half the votes of the first party, it is rewarded with a seat. However, neither of these cases utilizes the specific ethnic determination which characterizes the use of this mechanism in Mauritius.

Conclusion

The main argument in favor of all four explicitist approaches above is that they try to defuse ethnicity as a political issue, and to encourage the growth of other, competing cleavages, by making the recognition of ethnicity explicit in the electoral law. Yet because of this, they each suffer from the same fundamental drawback: each requires some official recognition and determination of group identity. Someone, somewhere, has to be able to determine who is and is not an Indian, a black, a scheduled caste member, and so on. A second major drawback is that such approaches assume that ethnic identities are immutable and enduring, and thus can contribute to the solidification of ethnic politics rather than its breakdown. Moreover, all the systems outlined above suffer from a distinct lack of flexibility: changes in the proportions of ethnic groups present in the community are not reflected in the legislature, which is effectively frozen in time from whenever the original determinations of group proportions were made. In Lebanon until 1990, for example, the ratio of parliamentary seats was fixed at six Christian for every five Muslim, which became a major issue of contention as the Muslim population grew more rapidly than the Christian one, and was consequently amended to a one-to-one ratio under the Taif Accords. While there may be some extremely deeply divided societies which demand such approaches (Lebanon appears to be one, and Bosnia may turn out to be another), in general most multiethnic societies need political institutions which help to break down the salience of ethnicity rather than predetermining it as the basis of electoral competition.

CONCLUSIONS

Divided societies, like Tolstoy's unhappy families, tend to be divided in different ways. This may seem like a simple or even simplistic statement, but it is surprising how often "one size fits all" conflict-managing packages are recommended for divided societies, usually by foreign "experts," without sufficient understanding of the structure of the conflict itself. As our earlier discussion of the typologies of conflict attempts to make clear, there are many variables in terms of the nature of a political conflict which will directly influence the optimum electoral system prescriptions. Table 1 presents a summary of the four electoral system options for conflict mediation outlined in the previous section, and the major examples of their application in divided societies around the world.

Having outlined and summarized these four major options, the following tables represent a first attempt to categorize some of these issues which need to be considered when attempting to implement one or another approach. While it is clear that constitutional choices such as electoral systems can have a substantive impact on the moderation or exacerbation of a conflict (indeed, for the "electoral engineering" approach typified by this paper, this is a fundamental precept), for policy makers the choice of electoral system is almost always dependent upon the nature of the conflict and of the society in question. In other words, the choice of appropriate electoral system is usually seen first and foremost as a response to a preexisting set of circumstances, which may then go on to affect the nature of those circumstances. For this reason, the following matrixes treat the choice of electoral system as the *dependent* variable, and the nature of the conflict as the *independent* variable, for the purposes of our analysis.

In the following tables, we look at the relationship between social structure, the nature of the conflict, and electoral system choice in order to determine whether there are any observed regularities that appear to influence or determine these choices. The systems we concentrate upon, as integral parts of the four "engineering packages" we identified in the section on Electoral Systems and Conflict Management are: list proportional representation (e.g., Belgium, Switzerland, and post-apartheid South Africa), the alternative vote (e.g., Papua New Guinea 1964-1975, and Fiji since 1997), the single transferable vote (e.g., Estonia in 1990, and Northern Ireland), and explicitist strategies such as separate communal voting rolls and mixed lists (e.g., Singapore, Lebanon, and Mauritius).

Nature of Group Identity

As noted earlier, it is appropriate to see the intensity of an individual's

TABLE 1 The Characteristics of System Choices Types

Type	List PR (Consociationalism)	AV (Centripetalism)	STV (Consensualism)	Communal Rolls, Party Block Vote (Explicitism)
Ethos	Proportional representation elections which lead to an inclusive legislature which includes all significant groups. Under a full consociational package, each group is represented in cabinet in proportion to their electoral support, and minority interests are protected through segmental autonomy and mutual vetoes.	Majority system with in-built incentives for interethnic party appeals. To maximize electoral prospects, parties need to cultivate the second preference votes from groups other than their own. There is a *centripetal* spin to the system where elites are encouraged to gravitate to the moderate multiethnic center. In ethnically mixed districts, majority threshold leads to strong incentives to gain support from other groups.	The electoral system delivers proportional results but also encourages politicians to appeal to the votes of members from other groups via secondary preferences. This can result in inclusive power-sharing between all significant political forces, but also in incentives for politicians to reach out to other groups for preference support.	System explicitly recognizes communal groups to give them (relatively fixed) institutional representation. Competition for power between ethnic groups is defused because the ratio of ethnic groups is fixed in advance. Electors must therefore make their voting choice on the basis of criteria other than ethnicity.
Examples	Switzerland, the Netherlands, South Africa 1994 (partially)	Papua New Guinea 1964-75, Fiji 1997- (partially)	Estonia 1990, Northern Ireland 1998- (partially)	Lebanon, Singapore, Mauritius (partially)

identification with any given group, and the nature of overall social group identity, as running along a continuum. Some conflictual identities are clearly more rigid than others, and a broad rule for electoral system design might be that the more rigid communal identification is, the higher the premium that should be placed on institutions which will represent "groups" in close approximation to their power and size. As identities become increasingly fluid and malleable, the more space there may be for electoral rules which encourage multiethnic voting coalitions and the representation of minority interests by candidates who may not be from that minority.

As Table 2 illustrates, large district closed list PR systems have been often used in societies where communal identity has been perceived to be hostile and rigid (e.g., South Africa, Bosnia, and Cyprus) while preference voting has been chosen for societies where identity was seen to be more fluid or at least open to cooperation with others (e.g., Fiji, Papua New Guinea). The exception to this rule has been the use of STV for various elections in Northern Ireland which is clearly a deeply divided society and where inter-ethnic vote transfers have not historically been a factor in conflict management (see Elliott, 1992). Finally, explicitist strategies are used in both high-intensity (Lebanon, Fiji) and low-intensity (Mauritius, New Zealand) conflicts, but it is instructive to note that in the latter two countries, where ethnic issues have become less sensitive, support for communal strategies has correspondingly declined.

Intensity of Conflict

There has been an ongoing debate among scholars of ethnic conflict as to the applicability of the various electoral engineering options to different levels of intensity of a conflict. On the one hand, advocates of consociationalism and list PR point to its use as a successful conflict-management tool in the divided societies of Western Europe, such as Belgium, the Netherlands, and Switzerland—societies which have become less conflictual over the course of this century (Lijphart, 1977). On the other hand, advocates of centripetal approaches point to the general failure of consociationalism in the developing world, arguing that it is the precisely the low level of conflicts in the divided societies of Western European cases which accounts for consociationalism's success there (Horowitz, 1985).

In the earlier discussion of the relationship between the intensity of a conflict and the most appropriate electoral system, we suggested that centripetal and consensual approaches based on AV or STV elections are likely to work best where there is a degree of fluidity to ethnic identities and lower levels of ethnic conflict, while approaches in which ethnicity

TABLE 2 Electoral System Choice and the Nature of Group Identity

Nature of Group Identity	List PR (Consociationalism)	AV (Centripetalism)	STV (Consensualism)	Communal Rolls, Party Block Vote (Explicitism)
Rigid	Bosnia 1996, Cyprus	Fiji 1997	Northern Ireland 1973, 1997	Lebanon, Fiji 1997 (communal rolls)
Intermediate	South Africa, Switzerland	Papua New Guinea 1964-75	Estonia 1990	New Zealand (Maori seats)
Fluid	The Netherlands	Australia	—	Mauritius

was more explicitly recognized (consociationalism and explicitism) may be more appropriate for the more intense conflicts. If we look at actual cases of electoral system choice in multiethnic societies (see Table 3), then it does appear that, outside the developed West, examples of conflict-mitigation packages based on list PR elections are concentrated at the high-intensity ends of the scale (e.g., Bosnia, South Africa, Cyprus), while centripetalism has been applied to societies divided with more moderate intensity (Papua New Guinea from 1964 to 1975 and most recently Fiji, which appears in the list twice, as its new constitution makes use of both a centripetal electoral system—AV in heterogeneous constituencies—and the explicitist device of communal-roll seats). "Extreme" intensity conflicts are classified as having occurred in those societies in which civil wars have been fought around issues of ethnicity and identity, such as Bosnia, Northern Ireland, Lebanon, and Sri Lanka.

Size, Number, and Distribution of Ethnic Groups

Possibly the most important contextual differences between the various systems choices become apparent when we examine the *size, number,* and *distribution* of ethnic groups. As explained earlier, centripetal approaches based on AV are likely to work best with a low to medium number of geographically intermixed groups, or with a very high number of geographically concentrated groups. Both of these social structures result in heterogeneous electoral districts, as does our "part concentrated, part intermixed" category, where larger districts utilizing STV should also be sufficiently heterogeneous for vote pooling to take place in many areas. Ethnic groups which are organized "semigeographically," such as Hispanic and Asian minorities in the United States, can also be represented via "the ethnic gerrymandering of amoeba-like districts" (Jenkins, 1994).

If we compare this with the situation where groups are geographically *concentrated,* then list PR systems are likely to be a more appropriate choice, as they do not rely on a geographically intermixed ethnic structure to work effectively and are capable of maintaining highly proportional results as the numbers of competing groups increase. Lijphart himself identifies the geographic concentration of ethnic groups as being a "favorable condition" for consociational democracy (Lijphart 1985). A highly segregated social structure is also often an indicator of a more intense inter-ethnic hostility. In the former Yugoslavia, for example, "ethnic cleansing" in the 1991-1995 war dramatically increased ethnic homogeneity in many regions. It is no surprise, then, that countries with a few large, geographically concentrated groups (Belgium, Switzerland, South Africa, much of post-Dayton Bosnia) have typically chosen PR electoral systems,

TABLE 3 Intensity of Conflict and Electoral System Choice

Intensity of Conflict	List PR (Consociationalism)	AV (Centripetalism)	STV (Consensualism)	Communal Rolls, Party Block Vote (Explicitism)
Low	Belgium, Switzerland, Spain	Australia	—	New Zealand (Maori seats), Mauritius
Moderate	Israel	PNG 1964-1975	Estonia 1990	Singapore
High	South Africa, Guyana	Fiji	—	India (scheduled castes), Fiji
Extreme	Bosnia, Cyprus, Sri Lanka	—	Northern Ireland	Lebanon

while countries with more intermixed populations were more likely to choose mixed or majoritarian models (pre-war Yugoslavia, India, Trinidad and Tobago, Fiji). It is interesting to note that the other model associated with more intense conflict, ethnically defined lists under a party block vote, has always been used in situations where ethnic groups are geographically interspersed (e.g., Lebanon, Singapore) rather than concentrated, as it enables candidate lists to be structured in such a way as to replicate the social structures of particular districts (such as in Lebanon).

Prescriptions for electoral engineering are thus heavily dependent on questions of social structure and, in particular, group demography. Clearly, we need to look more carefully at the *type* of ethnic division within a particular country or region. According to Lijphart, the optimal number of "segments" for a consociational approach to work is three or four, and conditions become progressively less favorable as more segments (i.e., groups) are added.[29] The centripetal approach, by contrast, requires a degree of proliferation of ethnic groups (or, at least, ethnic parties) to present the essential preconditions for vote-pooling to take place, and its chances for success will typically improve as the number of segments increase (Reilly, 1998a). The converse is also true: centripetal systems like AV are likely to result in majoritarian mono-ethnic dominance when applied in situations of group concentration, while list PR has had the effect of reinforcing ethnic parties when applied to intermixed societies like Guyana and Suriname.

Another factor is the relative size of ethnic groups: consociationalism favors groups of roughly equal size (although "bicommunal systems," in which two groups of approximately equal sizes coexist, can present one of most confrontationalist formulas of all);[30] while for centripetalism the crucial variable is the combination of size with the geographic concentration or dispersion of ethnic groups. In cases of group concentration, only highly fractionalized social structures can still exhibit the necessary degree of district-level heterogeneity to make centripetalism an effective strategy. In many cases, however, indigenous and/or tribal groups tend to display a strong tendency towards geographical concentration, but are not sufficiently fragmented to create heterogeneous districts. African minorities, for example, have been found to be more highly concentrated in single contiguous geographical areas than minorities in other regions, which means that many electoral constituencies and informal local power bases are dominated by a single ethnopolitical group (Scarritt, 1993). This has considerable implications for electoral engineers: it means that any system of election that relies on single-member electoral districts will likely produce "ethnic fiefdoms" at the local level. Minority representation and/or power-sharing under these conditions would probably require some form of multimember district system such as proportional representation.

Contrast this with the highly intermixed patterns of ethnic settlement found as a result of colonial settlement, labor importation and diaspora populations found in some Asia-Pacific (e.g., Singapore, Fiji, Malaysia) and Caribbean (Guyana, Suriname, Trinidad and Tobago) countries, in which members of various ethnic groups tend to be much more widely intermixed. Under such circumstances, many electoral districts are likely to be ethnically heterogeneous, so centripetal electoral strategies which make broad-based support a precondition for victory may well work to break down interethnic antagonisms and promote the development of broad, multiethnic parties. On such prosaic details rest much weightier prescriptions for the success or failure of consociational and centripetal approaches to the management of ethnic conflict.

Transitional Versus Consolidated Democracies

A final approach to electoral system choice is to ask whether the state in question is a transitional democracy, an established democracy, or a failed democracy. This gives us a quite different typology (Table 4). For one thing, almost all of the "extreme" intensity conflicts from Table 3— Bosnia, Sri Lanka, Northern Ireland, and Lebanon—suffered a breakdown in democracy under the specified system, which serves as a sobering reminder of the limits of constitutional engineering. Second, there is a clear regional concentration of electoral system choices: virtually all the countries of continental Europe, whether ethnically divided or not, use list PR systems (which are also common in Latin America and Southern Africa); AV systems are found exclusively in the South Pacific (Australia, pre-independence PNG, post-1997 Fiji, and Nauru); STV is used exclusively in countries which have had some colonial relationship with Britain (Ireland, both north and south; Malta; and in various jurisdictions in Australia); while explicitism is a strategy which, outside New Zealand, appears to be the near-exclusive preserve of the developing world (Fiji, Lebanon, Mauritius, India, etc.).

In a forthcoming work, Arend Lijphart identifies nine countries which can be classified as being both *established democracies* and *plural societies*: Belgium, Canada, India, Israel, Mauritius, Papua New Guinea, Spain, Switzerland, and Trinidad and Tobago (Lijphart, forthcoming). Again, the breakdown of these is illuminating: most "established democracy" examples of list PR elections for divided societies have taken place in relatively small industrialized countries, while all the examples of centripetalism and explicitism are in the developing world (Papua New Guinea, India, and Mauritius). No divided society in an established de-

TABLE 4 Nature of State and Electoral System Choice

Nature of Democracy	List PR (Consociationalism)	AV (Centripetalism)	STV (Consensualism)	Communal Rolls, Party Block Vote (Explicitism)
Transitional democracy	South Africa 1994-, Bosnia 1996	Fiji 1997-	Estonia 1990	Lebanon 1990-, Fiji 1997-
Established democracy	Belgium, Spain, Switzerland	Australia, PNG 1964-1975	—	Mauritius, India
Democratic failure	Sri Lanka 1983, Suriname 1980, Guyana 1980	—	Northern Ireland 1973	Lebanon 1975, Fiji 1987

mocracy outside the West uses PR, although PR has been a common choice in transitional democracies in Africa in recent years.

The final variable that may prove illuminating is whether breakdowns of democracy have occurred more or less under a particular system choice. As Table 4 suggests, advocates of different approaches can point to democratic successes and failures among divided societies. It is also the case, however, that countries such as Fiji, Lebanon, Northern Ireland, Sri Lanka, and others have persisted with (or reintroduced in modified form) the same electoral system design in place when democracy broke down. As discussed earlier, however, the bulk of new democracies in the post-war period simply adopted the electoral systems of their former colonists, evidencing equally unsatisfactory results across both majoritarian and proportional systems.

Conclusion

If the foregoing section suggests more randomness than regularity, it is still possible to isolate several factors that appear to be crucial when choosing between different models of electoral system design. First, the *intensity* of conflict does appear to have had an impact on the choice of electoral system for many divided societies. Specifically, the experience to date suggests that centripetal methods have been adopted in cases of more moderate conflicts and/or more fluid group identities, while list PR has tended to be adopted for transitional elections in more intensely conflictual situations. This fits with our earlier theoretical speculation that systems which require a degree of bargaining and cross-ethnic voting may be less realistic in extremely divided societies—where interethnic bargains, if any, may have to be made by elites alone—than in cases where there is a degree of fluidity to ethnic identities. This is why a system which combines elements of both approaches—such as STV—may well offer an attractive "middle road" position, combining as it does some incentives for vote-pooling with reasonably good proportionality. Unfortunately, the use of STV in divided societies has been extremely limited and inconclusive to date. Nonetheless, there is some encouraging evidence from Northern Ireland's 1998 elections, where STV formed part of a wider prescription for power-sharing between the Catholic and Protestant populations, that STV served to advantage the pro-agreement, non-sectarian center (Wilder, 1998).

The experience of systems in which ethnicity is explicitly recognized in the electoral system is somewhat contradictory. Both Lebanon and Fiji have suffered democratic breakdowns under such systems, but both have chosen to reintroduce elements of communalism in their new constitutions. It may well be that the value of such approaches lies in their ability to contain and manage a deep ethnic conflict until new cleavages arise to take their place. The experience of Mauritius is instructive in this regard: now that ethnicity is no longer a core political issue, the communal elements of the Mauritian electoral system, via ethnically designated "best loser" seats, are seen as a relic of times past (Mathur, 1997).

In terms of the four major electoral options for managing multiethnic conflicts, all have been successfully used in some divided societies, and all have suffered democratic failure at various points in time as well. But the respective needs of transitional versus consolidated democracies are often quite different. Put simply, the most important factor for democratic transition in electoral terms is usually a system that maximizes inclusiveness, is clearly fair to all parties, and presents minimal areas for potential preelection conflicts (such as the drawing of electoral boundaries)—goals that are usually best maximized by some form of regional or national list PR and which can lead to the election of a "grand" or "oversized" coalition government.

By contrast, the priorities of a consolidated democracy may be more concerned with crafting a system which gives rise to minimal winning coalition or single party governments, is accountable in both geographic and policy terms, and allows the voters to "throw out" a government if it does not perform to their satisfaction—goals that are enhanced by a system based, at least to some extent, upon small geographically defined electoral districts that does not entrench oversize coalition governments. South Africa, which successfully conducted its transitional 1994 election using a national-list PR system and a mandated "Government of National Unity," has moved away from power-sharing measures and may change to some form of constituency-based PR system for its next elections in 2004. The differences between the needs of transitional and consolidated democracies are represented diagramatically at Table 5.

ADVICE FOR POLICY MAKERS

There is no perfect electoral system, and no "right" way to approach the subject of electoral system design. The major criteria for designing electoral systems for all societies, not just divided ones, are sometimes in conflict with each other or even mutually exclusive. Devices that increase proportionality, such as increasing the number of seats to be elected in each district, may lessen other desirable characteristics, such as promoting geographic accountability between the electorate and the parliament. The electoral system designer must therefore go through a careful process of prioritizing which criteria are most important to the particular political context before moving on to assess which system will do the best job. For example, an ethnically divided state in Central Africa might want above

TABLE 5 Ideal Qualities of Electoral Institutions for Transitional and Consolidated Democracies

Transitional Democracy	Consolidated Democracy
• Inclusive	• Accountable
• Simple for voters to understand	• Enables voters to express more
• Fairness in results (proportionality)	sophisticated range of choice
• Minimize areas of conflict	• Ability to "throw the rascals out"
• Simple to run	• Responsive to electorate
• Transparent	• Promote sense of "ownership" of
• "Grand" or "oversized" coalition	political process among voters
governments	• "Minimal winning" coalitions or
	single-party governments

all to avoid excluding minority ethnic groups from representation in order to promote the legitimacy of the electoral process and avoid the perception that the electoral system is unfair. In contrast, while these issues would remain important, a fledgling democracy in a multiethnic state in Eastern Europe might have different priorities—e.g., to ensure that a government could efficiently enact legislation without fear of gridlock and that voters are able to remove discredited leaders if they so wish. How to prioritize among such competing criteria can only be the domain of the domestic actors involved in the constitutional design process.

Two levels of tension exist in the choice of electoral system options for divided societies. The first concerns those systems which place a premium on *representation* of minority groups (list PR and ethnically defined lists) compared to those which try to emphasize minority *influence* (AV and STV). As Horowitz has noted, "measures that will guarantee representation to a given ethnic or racial group may not foster the inclusion of that group's interest more broadly in the political process" (1991:165). The best option, of course, is to have both: representation of all significant groups, but in such a way as to maximize their influence and involvement in the policy-making process. This goal is best achieved by building both devices to achieve proportionality and incentives for interethnic accommodation into the electoral system itself. However, these goals are not always mutually compatible.

A second level of tension exists between those systems which rely on elite accommodation (especially list PR) and those which rely on the electorate at large for moderation (AV and STV). Where elites are likely to be more moderate than the electorate, then list PR enables the major parties to include candidates from various groups on their ticket. Where the electorate itself is the major engine of moderation, then AV and other systems which encourage vote pooling are likely to result in the election of more moderate leaders and more accommodative policies. When neither group is likely to display moderation, then ethnically mandated lists may need to be considered, as this provides the best way of "defusing" the salience of ethnicity as an electoral issue.

It should also be remembered that, although conflict-management packages based on consociationalism, centripetalism, consensualism, and explicitism do represent alternative approaches, they are not mutually exclusive. In fact, creative constitutional engineering that utilizes appropriate levers from a number of divergent approaches may well offer the optimum strategy in some cases. A good example of this is the 1997 constitutional settlement in Fiji. In 1987 Fiji experienced an armed coup on the part of the indigenous Fijian armed forces against an elected government dominated by Indo-Fijians, which resulted in the formulation of a racially weighted constitution which discriminated against Fiji's Indian population. After years of international condemnation and economic decline, a new constitution specifically designed to promote peaceful, multiethnic government was promulgated. This constitution mandated a centripetal approach to electoral competition (via the Alternative Vote), but also included provisions borrowed from consociationalism (mandated power sharing) and, more controversially, from explicitism (a partial continuation of the system of communal representation for Fijian, Indian, and "general" electors). The new constitution is thus a structure in which a high, or even a redundant, level of institutional levers for conflict management has been deliberately built into the system.

While Fiji's constitution-makers saw fit to make communal representation part of this new system, in general the comparative evidence to date suggests that *explicitist* approaches—ethnically mandated lists, communal rolls, racial gerrymandering, and the like—may serve artificially to sustain ethnic divisions in the political process rather than mitigating them. For this reason, we would counsel against their use in all but the most extreme cases of ethnic division. We would also recommend against systems that are overtly majoritarian in their operation: namely, the block vote and the two-round system. It is remarkable to note how many fledgling democracies in Africa, Asia, and the former Soviet Union use one or the other of these systems, considering their propensity to produce undesirable results. Both tend to reduce minority representation, and are thus unsurprisingly associated with authoritarian or other "unfree" regimes (Reynolds and Reilly, 1997:22). In addition, the Block Vote typically leads to single-party domination of parliaments and the elimination of opposition elements, while Two-Round systems place considerable strain on a state's electoral apparatus by having to run elections twice within a short space of time. The continuation of such systems points to the basic problem of inertia in any electoral reform.

Too often, constitutional drafters simply choose the electoral system they know best (often, in new democracies, the system of the former colonial power if there was one) rather than investigating the most appropriate alternatives. This does not mean we would necessarily advocate wholesale changes to existing electoral systems. In fact, the comparative experience of electoral reform to date suggests that moderate reforms that build on those things in an existing system which work well is often a better option than jumping to a completely new and unfamiliar system. What we do know is that there are several approaches to designing electoral systems for divided societies and that there is no single choice that is likely to be best in all cases. The optimal choice depends on several identifiable factors specific to each country, including its political history, the way and degree to which ethnicity is politicized, the intensity of conflict, and the demographic and geographic distribution of ethnic groups. While the combination of such variables in a given country gives us some useful pointers about electoral system design, it also can place considerable constraints upon constitutional engineers. The choice of electoral systems is always politically sensitive and always constrained by political considerations. Constitutional engineers in practice usually have limited room for maneuver. Nonetheless, despite such constraints, appropriate (and inappropriate) electoral system choices are powerful levers of democratic engineering, which inevitably have a marked influence on the future conduct of electoral politics.

REFERENCES

Anderson, Benedict. 1991. *Imagined Communities: Reflections on the Origin and Spread of Nationalism.* London: Verso.

Barczak, Monica. 1997. "Electoral Rules, Responsiveness, and Party Systems: Comparing Chile and Ecuador." Paper delivered at 1997 Annual Meeting of the American Political Science Association, Washington, D.C., August 28-31, 1997.

Barkan, Joel D. 1995. "Elections in Agrarian Societies." *Journal of Democracy* 6:106-116.

Birch, Sarah. 1997. "Ukraine: The Perils of Majoritarianism in a New Democracy." Pp. 48-50 in Andrew Reynolds and Ben Reilly, eds. *The International IDEA Handbook of Electoral System Design,* Stockholm: International Institute for Democracy and Electoral Assistance.

Carstairs, Andrew M. 1980. *A Short History of Electoral Systems in Western Europe.* London: George, Allen and Unwin.

Cliffe, Lionel, with Ray Bush, Jenny Lindsay, Brian Mokopakgosi, Donna Pankhurst, and Balefi Tsie. 1994. *The Transition to Independence in Namibia.* Boulder: Lynne Rienner.

Connors, Michael Kelly. 1996. "The Eclipse of Consociationalism in South Africa's Democratic Transition." *Democratization* 3:420-434.

Constitution Review Commission 1996. *The Fiji Islands: Towards a United Future.* Parliamentary Paper No. 34 of 1996. Suva: Parliament of Fiji.

Diamond, Larry. 1995. "Nigeria: The Uncivil Society and the Descent into Praetorianism." In *Politics in Developing Countries: Comparing Experiences with Democracy*, Larry Diamond, Juan Linz and S.M. Lipset, eds. Boulder: Lynne Rienner.

Diamond, Larry, Juan Linz, and S.M. Lipset, eds. 1995. *Politics in Developing Countries: Comparing Experiences with Democracy*. Boulder: Lynne Rienner

Diamond, Larry. 1996. "Towards Democratic Consolidation." Pp. 227-240 in *The Global Resurgence of Democracy*, Larry Diamond and Marc F. Plattner, eds. Baltimore and London: Johns Hopkins University Press.

de Silva, K.M. 1994. *Ethnic Diversity and Public Policies: Electoral Systems*. Geneva: UNRISD.

Elliott, Sydney. 1992. "Voting Systems and Political Parties in Northern Ireland." Pp. 76-93 in *Northern Ireland: Politics and the Constitution*, Brigid Hadfield, ed. Bristol, U.K.: Open University Press.

Elster, Jon. 1988. "Arguments for Constitutional Choice: Reflections on the Transition to Socialism." In *Constitutionalism and Democracy*, Jon Elster and Rune Slagstad, eds. Cambridge: Cambridge University Press.

Elster, Jon, and Rune Slagstad, eds. 1988. *Constitutionalism and Democracy*. Cambridge: Cambridge University Press.

Esman, M. 1994. *Ethnic Politics*. Ithaca and London: Cornell University Press.

Farrell, David M. 1997. *Comparing Electoral Systems*. London: Prentice Hall/Harvester Wheatsheaf.

Fearon, James D., and David D. Laitin. 1996. "Explaining Interethnic Cooperation." *American Political Science Review* 90:715-735.

Gallagher, Michael. 1997. "Ireland: The Archetypal Single Transferable Vote System." Pp. 85-87 in *The International IDEA Handbook of Electoral System Design*, Andrew Reynolds and Ben Reilly, eds. Stockholm: International Institute for Democracy and Electoral Assistance.

Geertz, Clifford. 1973. *The Interpretation of Cultures*. New York: Basic Books.

Grofman, Bernard, and Arend Lijphart, eds. 1986. *Electoral Laws and Their Political Consequences*. New York: Agathon Press.

Harris, Peter, and Ben Reilly, eds. 1998. *Democracy and Deep-Rooted Conflict: Options for Negotiators*. Stockholm: International IDEA.

Horowitz, Donald L. 1985. *Ethnic Groups in Conflict*. Berkeley: University of California Press.

Horowitz, Donald L. 1990. "Making Moderation Pay: The Comparative Politics of Ethnic Conflict Management." Pp. 451-475 in *Conflict and Peacemaking in Multiethnic Societies*, Joseph V. Montville, ed. New York: Lexington Books.

Horowitz, Donald L. 1991. *A Democratic South Africa? Constitutional Engineering in a Divided Society*. Berkeley: University of California Press.

Horowitz, Donald L. 1997. "Self-Determination: Politics, Philosophy, and Law." Pp. 421-463 in *Ethnicity and Group Rights*, I. Shapiro and W. Kymlicka, eds. New York and London: New York University Press.

Huntington, Samuel P. 1991. *The Third Wave: Democratization in the Late Twentieth Century*. Norman: University of Oklahoma Press.

Inter-Parliamentary Union. 1993. *Electoral Systems: A World-wide Comparative Study*. Geneva: Inter-Parliamentary Union.

Jenkins, Laura D. 1994. *Ethnic Accommodation Through Electoral Systems*. Geneva: UNRISD.

Kandeh, Jimmy D. 1992. "Politicization of Ethnic Identities in Sierra Leone." *African Studies Review* 35:81-99.

Kaspin, Deborah. 1995. "The Politics of Ethnicity in Malawi's Democratic Transition." *Journal of Modern African Studies* 33:595-620.

Koelble, Thomas. 1995. "The New Institutionalism in Political Science and Sociology." *Comparative Politics* 27:231-243.

Laitin, David. 1986. *Hegemony and Culture: Politics and Religious Change Among the Yoruba.* Chicago: University of Chicago Press.

Lakeman, Enid. 1974. *How Democracies Vote.* London: Faber and Faber.

Lewis, W. Arthur. 1965. *Politics in West Africa.* London: George Allen and Unwin.

Lijphart, Arend. 1977. *Democracy in Plural Societies: A Comparative Exploration.* New Haven: Yale University Press.

Lijphart, Arend. 1985. *Power Sharing in South Africa.* Policy Papers in International Affairs No. 24. Institute of International Studies, University of California, Berkeley.

Lijphart, Arend. 1990. "Electoral Systems, Party Systems and Conflict Management in Segmented Societies." Pp. 2-13 in *Critical Choices for South Africa: An Agenda for the 1990s,* R.A. Schreirer, ed. Cape Town: Oxford University Press.

Lijphart, Arend. 1991. "The Alternative Vote: A Realistic Alternative for South Africa?" *Politikon* 18:91-101.

Lijphart, Arend. 1994. *Electoral Systems and Party Systems: A Study of Twenty-Seven Democracies, 1945-1990.* New York: Oxford University Press.

Lijphart, Arend. 1995a. "Electoral Systems." Pp. 412-422 in *The Encyclopedia of Democracy,* S.M. Lipset. Washington D.C.: Congressional Quarterly Press.

Lijphart, Arend. 1995b. "Multiethnic Democracy." Pp. 853-865 in *The Encyclopedia of Democracy,* S.M. Lipset, ed. Washington D.C.: Congressional Quarterly Press.

Lijphart, Arend. 1997. "Disproportionality Under Alternative Voting: The Crucial—and Puzzling—Case of the Australian Senate Elections, 1919-1946." *Acta Politica* 32:9-24.

Lijphart, Arend. Forthcoming. *Patterns of Democracy: Government Forms and Performance in Thirty-Six Countries.* New Haven: Yale University Press.

Lijphart, Arend, and Bernard Grofman, eds. 1984. *Choosing an Electoral System: Issues and Alternatives.* New York: Praeger.

Lijphart, Arend, Rafael Lopez Pintor, and Yasunori Stone. 1986. "The Limited Vote and the Single Nontransferable Vote: Lessons from the Japanese and Spanish Examples." Pp. 154-169 in *Electoral Laws and their Political Consequences,* B. Grofman and A. Lijphart, eds. New York: Agathon Press.

MacBeth, John. 1998. "Dawn of a New Age." *Far Eastern Economic Review* (17 September):24-28.

Madden, A.F. 1980. "'Not for export': The Westminster Model of Government and British Colonial Practice." In *The First British Commonwealth: Essays in Honour of Nicholas Mansergh,* N. Hillmer and P. Wigley, eds. London: Frank Cass.

Mansfield, Edward D., and Jack Snyder. 1995. "Democratization and War." *Foreign Affairs* 74:79-97.

March, James, and Johan Olsen. 1984. "The New Institutionalism: Organizational Factors in Political Life." *American Political Science Review* 78:734-749.

Mathur, Raj. 1997. "Parliamentary Representation of Minority Communities: The Mauritian Experience." *Africa Today* 44:61-77.

Mattes, Robert B. 1995. *The Election Book: Judgement and Choice in South Africa's 1994 Elections.* Cape Town: IDASA Public Information Centre.

Milne, R.S. 1982. *Politics in Ethnically Bipolar States.* Vancouver: University of British Columbia Press.

Nagata, Judith. 1979. "Review of Lijphart's *Democracy in Plural Societies.*" *International Journal* 34:505-506.

Newman, Saul. 1991. "Does Modernization Breed Ethnic Political Conflict?" *World Politics* 43:451-478.

Price, Robert M. 1995. "Civic Versus Ethnic: Ethnicity and Political Community in Post-Apartheid South Africa." Unpublished paper.

Przeworski, A. 1991. *Democracy and the Market: Political and Economic Reforms in Eastern Europe and Latin America.* Cambridge: Cambridge University Press.

Putnam, Robert D., with Robert Leonardi and Raffaella Y. Nanetti. 1993. *Making Democracy Work: Civic Traditions in Modern Italy.* Princeton: Princeton University Press.

Rae, Douglas W. 1967. *The Political Consequences of Electoral Laws.* New Haven: Yale University Press.

Reid, Ann. 1993. "Conflict Resolution in Africa: Lessons from Angola." INR Foreign Affairs Brief. Washington D.C.: US Department of State.

Reilly, Ben. 1997a. "The Alternative Vote and Ethnic Accommodation: New Evidence from Papua New Guinea." *Electoral Studies* 16:1-11.

Reilly, Ben. 1997b. "Preferential Voting and Political Engineering: A Comparative Study." *Journal of Commonwealth and Comparative Studies* 35:1-19.

Reilly, Ben. 1998a. "Constitutional Engineering in Divided Societies: Papua New Guinea in Comparative Perspective." Ph.D. dissertation, Australian National University, Canberra.

Reilly, Ben. 1998b. "With No Melting Pot, a Recipe for Failure in Bosnia." *International Herald Tribune*, 12-13 September, p.6.

Reilly, Ben, and Michael Maley. 1999. "The Single Transferable Vote and the Alternative Vote Compared." In *STV in Comparative Perspective*, Shaun Bowler and Bernard Grofman, eds. Ann Arbor: University of Michigan Press.

Reynolds, Andrew, ed. 1994. *Election '94: South Africa—An Analysis of the Results, Campaigns, and Future Prospects.* New York: St. Martin's Press.

Reynolds, Andrew. 1995. "The Case for Proportionality." *Journal of Democracy* 6:117-124.

Reynolds, Andrew. 1996. "Electoral Systems and Democratic Consolidation in Southern Africa." Ph.D. dissertation, University of California at San Diego.

Reynolds, Andrew, and Ben Reilly. 1997. *The International IDEA Handbook of Electoral System Design.* Stockholm: International Institute for Democracy and Electoral Assistance.

Reynolds, Andrew, and Jørgen Elklit. 1997. "Jordan: Electoral System Design in the Arab World." In *The International IDEA Handbook of Electoral System Design*, Andrew Reynolds and Ben Reilly, eds. Stockholm: International Institute for Democracy and Electoral Assistance.

Reynolds, Andrew, and Timothy D. Sisk. 1998. "Elections, Electoral Systems, and Conflict Management." In *Elections and Conflict Resolution in Africa*, Timothy Sisk and Andrew Reynolds, eds. Washington, D.C.: United States Institute of Peace Press.

Rokkan, Stein. 1970. *Citizens, Elections, Parties: Approaches to the Comparative Study of the Processes of Development.* Oslo: Universitetsforlaget.

Rose, Richard. 1976. *Northern Ireland: A Time of Choice.* Washington D.C.: American Enterprise Institute.

Rule, Wilma, and Joseph Zimmerman, eds. 1994. *Electoral Systems in Comparative Perspective: Their Impact on Women and Minorities.* Westport, Conn.: Greenwood.

Sartori, Giovanni. 1968. "Political Development and Political Engineering." *Public Policy* 17:261-298.

Sartori, Giovanni. 1994. *Comparative Constitutional Engineering: An Inquiry Into Structures, Incentives, and Outcomes.* New York: Columbia University Press.

Scarritt, James R. 1993. "Communal Conflict and Contention for Power in Africa South of the Sahara." In *Minorities at Risk*, T. R. Gurr, ed. Washington, D.C.: United States Institute of Peace Press.

Scarritt, James R., and Shaheen Mozaffar. 1996. "The Potential for Sustainable Democracy in Africa." Paper presented at the International Studies Association, San Diego, April 19, 1996.

Shils, Edward 1957. "Primordial, Personal, Sacred, and Civil Ties." *British Journal of Sociology* 8:130-145.

Sisk, Timothy D. 1995. *Democratization in South Africa: The Elusive Social Contract*. Princeton: Princeton University Press.

Sisk, Timothy D. 1996. *Power Sharing and International Mediation in Ethnic Conflicts*. Washington, D.C.: United States Institute of Peace Press.

Taagepera, Rein. 1990. "The Baltic States." *Electoral Studies* 9:303-311.

Taagepera, Rein. 1998. "How Electoral Systems Matter for Democratization." *Democratization* 5(3):68-91.

Taagepera, Rein, and Matthew S. Shugart. 1989. *Seats and Votes: The Effects and Determinants of Electoral Systems*. New Haven: Yale University Press.

Vengroff, Richard. 1994. "The Impact of Electoral System on the Transition to Democracy in Africa: The Case of Mali." *Electoral Studies* 13:29-37.

Wilder, Paul. 1998. "A Pluralist Parliament for a Pluralist People? The New Northern Ireland Assembly Elections, 25 June 1998." *Representation* 35:97-105.

Young, Crawford. 1976. *The Politics of Cultural Pluralism*. Madison: University of Wisconsin Press.

NOTES

[1]Ben Reilly is a Senior Programme Officer at the International Institute for Democracy and Electoral Assistance based in Stockholm, Sweden. Andrew Reynolds is an Assistant Professor in the Department of Government and International Studies at the University of Notre Dame, USA.

[2]See March and Olsen, 1984:747; and Koelble, 1995:232.

[3]See Prezworski, 1991: 10-14.

[4]See also Putnam, 1993.

[5]Sartori, 1968:273.

[6]Diamond, 1996:238.

[7]Diamond, 1996:239.

[8]Esman, 1994:14.

[9]Crawford Young also notes that the Ghanaian elections of 1996 were another example of substantial nonethnic block voting. Only the Ewe community could be categorized as "ethnic voters."

[10]Crawford Young, however, argues that "95 percent of whites voted for the NP, the IFP drew its votes heavily from Zulu, and the Colored vote was importantly shaped by the communal insecurities and concerns of that group."

[11]Lijphart, 1995b:853.

[12]In many African states, urbanization has led to ethnic intermixing. Mines and plantations are also more likely to have multiethnic workforces and thus communities.

[13]We are indebted to Crawford Young for pointing this out.

[14]For example, South Africa used a classically proportional electoral system for its first democratic elections of 1994, and with 62.65 percent of the popular vote the African National Congress (ANC) won 63 percent of the national seats. The electoral system was highly proportional, and the number of wasted votes (i.e., those which were cast for parties who did not win seats in the Assembly) was only 0.8 percent of the total (see Reynolds, 1994). However, under some circumstances nonproportional electoral systems (such as FPTP) can accidentally give rise to relatively proportional overall results. This was the case in a third Southern African country, Malawi, in 1994. In that election the leading party, the United Democratic Front won 48 percent of the seats with 46 percent of the votes, the Malawian Congress Party won 32 percent of the seats with 34 percent of the votes, and the

Alliance for Democracy won 20 percent of the seats with 19 percent of the votes. The overall level of proportionality was high, but the clue that this was not inherently a proportional system, and so cannot be categorized as such, was that the wasted votes still amounted to almost one-quarter of all votes cast.

[15]It must be noted however that the party system fragmentation of 1919-1933 was not a direct result of the PR system adopted from post-Great War Germany as party fragmentation was equally high and problematic under the pre-1919 two-round German electoral system. As Lakeman notes, the number of parties in the Reichstag in 1912 was 21, while during Hitler's rise to power in the early 1930s the party system had coalesced to four or five major blocks (Lakeman, 1974:209).

[16]Madden, 1980:20.

[17]Most notably in times of war, as in Britain, and times of internal upheaval, as in West Germany in the 1970s.

[18]Lijphart, 1990:11.

[19]For example, the South African National Assembly elected in 1994 was 52 percent black (11 percent Zulu, the rest of Xhosa, Sotho, Venda, Tswana, Pedi, Swazi, Shangaan, and Ndebele extraction), 32 percent white (one-third English, two-thirds Afrikaans), 7 percent Colored and 8 percent Indian. And the Namibian parliament is similarly diverse, with representatives from the Ovambo, Damara, Herero, Nama, Baster, and white (English and German speaking) communities (see Reynolds, 1995).

[20]See Rule and Zimmerman, 1994 and the Inter-Parliamentary Union, 1993.

[21]See Reynolds, 1996.

[22]See Horowitz, 1991:140-141.

[23]Connors argues that in South Africa consociationalism "rather than mitigating ethnic conflict, could only wittingly or unwittingly provide a basis for ethnic mobilization by providing segmental leaders with a permanent platform" (1996:426).

[24]Horowitz, 1990:471.

[25]Sisk, 1996:62.

[26]Scarritt, 1993:256

[27]Rose, 1976:78.

[28]See Taagepera, 1990.

[29]Lijphart, 1977:56.

[30]See Milne, 1982.